Hunger and Happiness

Feeding the Hungry,
Nourishing Our Souls

L. Shannon Jung

Augsburg Books
MINNEAPOLIS

HUNGER AND HAPPINESS
Feeding the Hungry, Nourishing Our Souls

Cover image: Diamond Sky Images
Cover design: Laurie Ingram
Book design: PerfecType, Nashville, TN

Library of Congress Cataloging-in-Publication Data

Jung, L. Shannon (Loyle Shannon), 1943-
  Hunger and happiness : feeding the hungry, nourishing our souls / L. Shannon Jung.
    p. cm.
  Includes bibliographical references (p.   ).
  ISBN 978-0-8066-7060-7 (alk. paper)
  1. Hunger—Religious aspects—Christianity. 2. Happiness—Religious aspects—Christianity. I. Title.
  BR115.H86J86 2009
  261.8'326--dc22
                                    2009011774

Manufactured in the U.S.A.

13 12 11 10 09   1 2 3 4 5 6 7 8 9 10

We cannot be fully nourished in the depths of our being if we try to isolate ourselves individually or if we seek to deprive others of their share by increasing our own; for the food that we eat nourishes us in both our souls and our bodies. To eat alone is to be starved in some part of our being. . . .

Perhaps our greatest resource for peace is in an awareness that we enrich ourselves when we share our possessions with others. We discover peace when we learn to esteem those goods whereby we benefit ourselves in proportion as we give them to others.

Thomas Berry

● ● ●

The only way to make people doubt, even for a minute, the inevitability of their course in life is to show them that they are being cheated of the truest happiness.

Bill McKibben

CONTENTS

Acknowledgments   vii
Introduction: Hunger amid Plenty   1

1. How Could Cheap Food Be a Bad Thing?   15
2. Healthy Food, Healthy Humans   41
3. Appropriations and the Earth Community   57
4. Cheap Food, Rural Communities, and Farming   75
5. Losing and Refinding Our Spiritual Selves   93
6. How Can We Reverse Complicity and
   Nourish Our Souls?   115

Conclusion   135
Notes   139
Index   149

ACKNOWLEDGMENTS

Is it appropriate to thank people in advance? If so, let me thank those people who read this book, who recognize themselves as I recognize myself in it, and then realize that doing something about hunger—both physical and spiritual—is key to their own nourishment. Let me also thank the Saint Paul students who are about to embark on my Theology of Growing and Eating course.

Turning to those who have already contributed much to this effort, I acknowledge the many emails I get that have pointed in this or that direction, that thank me or redirect me or make suggestions. My email address is shannon.jung@spst.edu, and feedback—as the Wheaties box says—is the breakfast of champions.

Any number of people have given me a chance to try out some of the ideas that appear here. Let me name some of the places that helped me refine these ideas: Columbia Theological Seminary; Cambridge University—Society for the Study of Christian Ethics; the Society of Christian Ethics—my professional home; Hiram College and Jon Moody; Concordia College and Arland Jacobson and the Religion Department there;

Saint Paul School of Theology; and the University of Dubuque and Wartburg seminaries.

A number of churches: Parkville Presbyterian—an exceedingly hospitable church and my parish; Saint Andrews Disciples; Church of the Resurrection (Episcopalian); Central United Methodist, and a lot of United Methodist and Presbyterian churches.

Pieces of this book in different forms have appeared in *The Lutheran*, *Rural Life* (National Catholic Rural Life Conference journal), *Horizons* (Presbyterian Women's magazine), and *atthispoint.edu* (Columbia Seminary online journal).

People: Steven Miller, of Bread for the World; my Saint Paul colleagues Jeanne Hoeft, Robert Martin, Harold Washington, Mike Graves, and now—oh, blessed day—my colleague of long standing, Dr. Patricia Beattie Jung. Joan Fumetti of Foods Resource Bank, the crew at the Kansas City Food Policy Coalition, the good farmers of my CSA operating as Good Natured Farms. I really appreciate Dr. Nancy Barry's expert eye in critiquing writing. Students who were very helpful include Amanda Lamb Ross and Morgan Whitaker.

Two of the editors at Augsburg Fortress have been extraordinary. Susan Johnson has been a rare combination of attentive, skillful, nice, and incisive. Michael West has contributed his wit and wisdom.

This book is dedicated to the three new members of our little tribe who now share the table, which has become a great deal messier. I am not talking about your eating habits, Cara Jung, but about Rowan Jung and Marissa Jung.

Finally, of course, the proof of the pudding is in the eating. Thus, I welcome your comments on this food and hope that we can together reach out and decrease our hunger and the hunger of the world. No reason not to delight while sharing, though!

INTRODUCTION:
HUNGER AMID PLENTY

The questions that confront us in a world of hunger are many and pressing—the lives of countless men, women, and children are at stake:

- Why, in a world where there is so much food, such an abundance, is there starvation?
- How does the global food system of production and distribution benefit some at the great expense of others?
- In what ways are the affluent complicit in the poverty and hunger of others?
- Why aren't the affluent who have an abundance of material goods any happier?
- Why do we cherish and safeguard our possessions so vigorously in the face of others' lack and suffering?
- If we live in a world of abundance and many share the belief that all should have access to that abundance—or at least have a sufficiency—why isn't that the case?
- What are the economic, political, and spiritual obstacles to shared abundance?

Obviously, these are social, economic, and political questions, but at the same time they are spiritual questions. I'm betting that, whatever your official religious beliefs, these questions bother you as they bother me. We will address them together in the pages of this book.

The question of abundance

When we hear the word *abundance*, we usually think of *material* abundance, such as food and water, shelter, clothing, access to health care. These are important, indeed critical for human well-being, but they are not sufficient for human well-being. When considering human well-being, we need to expand our understanding of abundance to include *spiritual* abundance along with material abundance. Spiritual abundance includes such things as friendship, love, gratitude, appreciation, and generosity. Indeed, the presence in one's life of what the apostle Paul called the "fruit of the Spirit"—love, joy, peace, patience, kindness, generosity, faithfulness, gentleness, and self-control (Gal. 5:22-23)—points to a spiritual abundance, apart from which material abundance is rarely meaningful or satisfying.

In terms of material abundance, there is enough to go around. That is the first assertion of this book. Without increasing spiritual abundance, however, it (1) won't go around and (2) won't bring happiness to those who have access to it. That is the second assertion, and the one that we will explore.

The Bible supports the belief that God is a God of abundance and that the world is divinely created for the well-being, even flourishing, of all creatures. Just read Psalm 104, in particular these verses:

You cause the grass to grow for the cattle,
   and plants for people to use,
to bring forth food from the earth,
   and wine to gladden the human heart,
oil to make the face shine,
   and bread to strengthen the human heart. (vv. 14-15)

And yet there are close to two billion people on this beautiful, rich, abundantly fruitful planet who do not get enough food, let alone experience the abundance that God provides. Abundance is not their reality, and it is difficult to imagine that they could imagine it ever being their reality.

Many of the affluent, those with easy access to the planet's abundant provision, believe more in scarcity than they do in abundance. This belief leads to the assumption that abundance is an ideal, not a reality—but an ideal to be strived for. If abundance is understood as only an ideal to be strived for, then it is easy to accept as "normal" that while some may experience abundance, many will not. As a person of faith in a God of abundance, I reject both a belief in scarcity and its related belief that hunger is understandable—if deplorable—for billions of people. Hunger amid plenty is neither necessary nor acceptable. Providing access to the abundant provisions of this planet to those who suffer from a lack of the material necessities of life is indeed a challenge, but not an intractable one. To meet the challenge, we all—but particularly the affluent—will need to access the spiritual abundance that gives meaning and purpose, satisfaction and joy (read happiness) to human life.

As I write this book, our nation's economy—and the global economy—has slipped into a severe recession and may be on the way to the greatest depression since the Great Depression in the 1930s. The economic meltdown has done much to reinforce the belief in scarcity, a belief that gives rise to the fear that there will not be enough for me/us. Such fear leads to greed, to hoarding, to holding at arm's length those who *seem* to threaten our getting "enough." Add this to the fact that we live in a society obsessed with work and wealth, consumption and possession as the source of happiness, and it is an easy step to blame the victim: the poor are poor and hungry because they lack the will or ability to "succeed" in what is seen as the zero-sum game of national and global economics.

We are spiritually malnourished. The zero-sum economic game in which abundance for some must be matched by scarcity for others has not led to true happiness or a sense of well-being for those who seem to be "winning" the game. Many of us feel as though we are on the wrong path. This book will suggest a different path.

Starting assertions

At this point we can make certain assertions that will guide our reflections on "hunger and happiness":

- God has created the world and humankind in such a way that there is an abundance of the material necessities of life and an abundance of the spiritual necessities of life.
- That abundance, we believe, should be shared by all—no exceptions.
- But some things block that kind of sharing.

Identifying the things that block access to abundance—and thus human happiness—is both a spiritual and an eminently practical task, and one that also bears on public policies that impact global hunger. There are social, economic, and political questions to be addressed—and there are faith questions to be dealt with.

Faith and hunger

The Christian tradition sees human hunger and suffering—both down the street and abroad—as a scandal. Other faith traditions, including Islam, Judaism, and Buddhism, also see hunger as a scandal, and the alleviation of hunger as a spiritual necessity. For example:

- In Matthew 25:35-45, Jesus tells his followers that when they give food to the hungry, they are giving food to him, and when they deny food to the hungry, they are denying him
- Islam makes it obligatory on every Muslim to pay a "tax," called *Zakat*, on their accumulated wealth. The money collected from the *Zakat* is to be distributed to the poor and hungry.[1]
- In *Midrash Tannaim*, on Numbers 28:2 in the Hebrew Scriptures, God says to Israel, "'My children, whenever you give sustenance to the poor, I impute it to you as though you gave sustenance to Me.'" Does God then eat and drink? No, but whenever you give food to the poor, God accounts it to you as if you gave food to God."
- In *Vinaya Mahavagga* 8.26.3, the Buddha tells his followers that they must tend to each other's needs, and in so doing, they tend to the Buddha.

In all of these faith traditions, caring for others, sharing material abundance, connects one to the Ultimate, and to ultimate meaning. It brings the happiness that we long for but find so elusive.[2]

Americans generally do not seem to be very happy people. We spend billions on prescription tranquilizers and drugs to fight depression. We suffer from obsessive-compulsive and addictive behaviors. We buy whatever marketers tell us will make us happy, but it rarely does. The prophet Isaiah's question to the Israelites is a good question for us: "Why do you spend your money for that which is not bread, and your labor for that which does not satisfy?" (Isa. 55:2).

When we consider the question of why U.S. citizens aren't any happier, we are dealing with more than questions of psychology or questions of chemical imbalances. We are also dealing with faith questions. What is the purpose of our lives? Why do we exist? Are we living out what we are for? Is this all there is? What will produce that deep sense of human well-being that will satisfy us, fill us up, enable us to live with joy? What will satiate those hungers we seek to satisfy with alcohol, diversions, food, drugs, and the like? These are spiritual questions that are not limited to any one faith tradition. As we shall see, these questions have something to do with our approach to the reality of hunger in a world of plenty. Indeed, perhaps some of the unhappiness of the American people—particularly people of faith—stems from the knowledge of our complicity[3] in the hunger of others.

Happiness and affluence

Before going further, it might be good to define two key terms. I am using the word *happiness* to point to the experience of "profound spiritual well-being." The quest for happiness is the quest for a deep sense of purpose in our lives that is grounded in an *inner* sense of communion with God and with the neighbor. Happiness comes with the certainty that we are seeking those things that make for peace and affirm the dignity and equality of all people as beloved children of God. This has nothing to do with the transient feelings of happiness that come from the momentary gratification of our desires by things outside our-selves. It has everything to do with an inner experience of one-ness with God and all that God has created.

When I speak of *affluence*, I am not speaking about the Warren Buffets and Bill Gates of the world. Rather, I use the term to refer to anyone who has a median standard of living in the United States. That translates into around $50,000 in annual income for a household. While that may sound pretty low to us, to those living in poverty in our own country and to the major-ity of people in the developing world, it is fabulous wealth. The "affluent" are those of us who are living comfortably; relative to the rest of the people in the world, *we have enough*.

This book is addressed to those of us who enjoy a median or higher income in the United States and other affluent coun-tries. What I am proposing is that we look carefully and hon-estly at the way our food policies (usually referred to as "cheap food" policies) have produced hunger and malnutrition among the poor while decreasing our own sense of spiritual well-being (deep-seated happiness). After all, how can we be happy in a world where there are so many hungry people, especially when we know that we are complicit in their hunger?

The global food system that we enjoy in the United States, Western Europe, Japan, and Australia comes at the expense of others in our own countries and around the world. We cannot enjoy the benefits of this system so long as we know that we are complicit in others' suffering. Their physical hunger is joined to our spiritual hunger. To lessen our spiritual hunger, we need to work to lessen their physical hunger.

Hunger and happiness are clearly linked. As long as peo-ple anywhere are hungry for food, true happiness and spiritual well-being will elude us. My sense of a lack of well-being comes from knowing that many people do not have enough and their lack of enough is tied to my having too much, or at least more than I need for a good, secure, meaningful life. And that is the crux of the matter I am addressing in this book—hunger and happiness.[4] Alleviate the former and find the latter.

Something can be done

The problem of hunger can seem overwhelming. Billions of people worldwide live in extreme poverty, and we clearly benefit from their poverty and hunger. It is all too easy to take a "there's nothing we can do about it" attitude. Such an attitude, of course, can become an excuse for not trying to do anything about it.

If we are to address the hunger issue, we need some hope that such injustices can be resisted successfully. Without the hope that suffering can be alleviated, the challenge of addressing it appears daunting to the point of impossibility. Without hope, action seems destined to futility. But there are grounds for hope. One can draw from history examples of ordinary people who recognized that they were, to some degree, implicated in the system that caused suffering for others, and who took successful action to halt injustice and bring about positive change. Many of these people acted out of their belief that their own God-given abundance compelled them to act against injustices from which they were benefiting. Others acted out of non-faith-based humanitarian motives. They all believed that something could be done.

Standing against slavery

In 1787, eleven thousand people in Manchester, England, began a movement that would succeed in stopping the slave trade. They joined an uphill battle against slavery, an institution that benefited them considerably. This campaign put their livelihood at risk since Manchester was a major processing center for the cotton that was produced by slave labor. Slavery also produced the sugar, wheat, barley, corn, salt, and rice enjoyed by both the workers and the affluent.

These were ordinary people, men and women whose livelihood and kitchen tables were tied to and benefited from the slave trade, and yet they worked to stop it. "Women especially, though greatly constrained by law and convention, supported the movement, contributed needlework with antislavery images and inscriptions ('Am I Not a Woman and a Sister?') and refused to buy sugar (slave-grown in the West Indies)."[5] These eleven thousand ordinary citizens did not simply blame slave traders from Liverpool, African tribes, London merchants, or southern U.S. and West Indies plantations. They recognized their own complicity and took steps to end it.

Thomas Pogge, a political philosopher at Columbia, suggests that they did not see their effort as super heroic. "We know about slavery," he projects them as saying; "we know that the cotton we touch every day has been planted and gathered by slaves. We know that ships flying our country's flag are carrying slaves across the Atlantic. We know we are part of this injustice and we know we must try to put a stop to it—for the sake of our black brothers and sisters and also for the sake of our country. We understand that success is unlikely and may be impossible. But we know that we must make the attempt."[6] They understood their role in the misery inflicted across a vast ocean and how they benefited from that misery. Something could be done and they did it.

Immokalee poverty and Taco Bell

There are those who would say that there are still slave wages in this country. The Coalition of Immokalee Workers (CIW), a community-based organization of Hispanic, Haitian, and Mayan Indian immigrants, accused Burger King, Taco Bell, McDonald's, and other fast food chains of abusing agricultural workers in Florida's growing fields. The CIW's Anti-Slavery Campaign is a worker-based approach to eliminate the practice of holding tomato and orange pickers in "debt bondage." They provide a combination of outreach to abused workers, investigation of abuse, and worker-to-worker counseling in order to combat already-existing poverty.

The CIW seeks to eliminate the market conditions that allow modern-day exploitation to flourish. They document how major food-buying corporations benefit from the exploitation of U.S. farmworkers (and keep consumer prices low). The CIW believes that the ultimate solution to modern-day slavery in agribusiness lies on the "demand side" of the U.S. produce market—the major food-buying corporations that profit from the artificially low cost of U.S. produce picked by workers in sweatshop conditions. The Coalition encouraged U.S. consumers who buy from Burger King, Taco Bell, and McDonald's to boycott those restaurants. Partnering with the Coalition is the Alliance for Fair Food, a network of human rights, religious, student, labor, and grassroots organizations.[7] The Alliance promotes principles and practices of socially responsible purchasing in the corporate food industry that advance and ensure the human rights of farmworkers who are at the bottom of corporate supply chains.

Recognizing the ways in which they, as consumers of fast food, benefit from cheap food grown by those who live in squalid conditions and are paid less than minimum wage, members of many churches endorsed the boycott and called for negotiations between Taco Bell, its tomato suppliers, and CIW representatives. The boycott led to a groundbreaking agreement that improved farmworker wages, guaranteed transparency in Taco Bell's tomato supply chain, and established the first code of conduct for Florida agricultural suppliers that guarantees a meaningful role for farmworkers in the protection of their own rights. Now McDonald's, Burger King, and Wendy's have joined Taco Bell in raising the price they pay for produce.[8] Again, ordinary people saw what could be done and they did it.

Reaching out with the Foods Resource Bank

One of my favorite examples of groups that feel drawn to do something to relieve the hunger and poor living conditions of people in countries around the world is the Foods Resource Bank (FRB).[9] That organization's genius is that it links people with many different resources to work toward assuaging world hunger.

People in rural congregations love Foods Resource Bank because it forms a direct link between what they know best— food and how to grow it—and those who need it most. People in rural congregations—often a single farmer or group of land-owners—donate a plot of land (which may be as small as an acre) and agree to grow a crop.

Urban church members donate the money for seeds and other needs, and even, in some cases, for land rental. A youth group, for example, may hold a fund-raiser to contribute money to the project; the farmer or farmers plant and tend the crop. When the crop is ready, both urban and rural groups come together for a harvest festival; the younger kids get to ride the combines, pet the calves, and see the harvesting. There is a community meal, the crop is sold, and the proceeds are donated to a global development project, either through a denominational hunger agency, an international Foods Resource Bank project, or a global development project selected by the churches themselves.

Fordham University theologian Tom Beaudoin sums up the dilemma that FRB is designed to address:

> We live with the knowledge and helpless feeling that someone somewhere may be suffering because of the way that the coffee we savor or the clothes we enjoy are produced, and we are too busy, tired, or already have enough of our own "issues" to even begin to do anything about it.[10]

FRB offers us a way to begin to do something about it. Penny Lauritzen, a certified financial planner from Lanark, Illinois, and an FRB volunteer uses a quote to describe her motivation:

> If I put myself in a long line with the people of the world—from the wealthiest, materially, to the poorest—I will always fall somewhere in between. Poverty and wealth tend to be relative, depending on where I am in the line. But what is important is the direction I choose to look and walk towards in this line. If I am always looking to the wealthy end, I am going to think I am poor and feel I need more. But if I work on turning myself around to look, though sometimes scary, in the opposite direction to those who have less, my life can be transformed. Values of community, sharing, gratitude and relationship will become more important.[11]

There are many stories of ordinary people who see what needs to be done, who see what can be done, and set about doing it. In their stories there is hope for the rest of us that hunger can be decreased and spiritual well-being increased. The purpose of this book is to name the problem, see our complicity in it, and work for change.

The plan of this book

Most of the chapters in this book will begin by describing a particular aspect of the hunger/well-being dynamic. Then the discussion will move to consider the ways in which our own standard of living is supported at the expense of others. Next we will consider wisdom from the social-scientific study of the psychology of happiness and explore how the material benefit we receive might in fact redound to our loss of well-being. Each chapter will then offer a theological perspective on the aspect of the food issue under discussion. That will be followed by an assessment of the moral implications of the chapter's topic, some possible remedies that could increase our spiritual well-being and decrease the physical hunger on the planet, and, finally, some questions to ponder. It takes awhile for food to be digested; in a similar way, it takes time to "digest" what we read. The questions at the conclusion of each chapter are designed to assist with the process of integrating and digesting. Some ask for your thoughts, while others are about your feelings or about actions you might take.

The last chapter will break this pattern. It will address what we can do in concrete and specific ways as individuals and as members of organizations, such as faith communities, to move beyond complicity toward greater well-being for ourselves, for others, and for our planet.

1

How Could Cheap Food Be a Bad Thing?

Some time ago, I addressed a group of college students on hunger issues. I had, somewhat facetiously, titled my lecture "Can the Affluent Be Saved?" My point was to talk about how our own health depends on confessing our complicity in appropriating the advantages that come to us at other people's expense—largely indirectly and unintentionally, but still unequivocally.

The students were well fed and privileged, and I wondered if they could *feel* what I was talking about. I doubted it. They had been born into a system that produces harm for many people while working to the advantage of the comfortable. Growing up on the privileged side of the American (and global) food system, these young people were understandably unaware, and largely uninterested, in their complicity in the suffering caused by hunger. I am not being accusatory. Those students (like most privileged Americans) did not mean anyone any harm, but they were unavoidably living within a system that causes harm. The first steps for those students (and for the rest of us) in attempting to undo the harm are (1) seeing and acknowledging complicity, (2) becoming aware of the harm caused, (3) and becoming involved in compassion-driven action that challenges and changes the system. Hence the reason for this book—to encourage all of us to take those first steps.

Why does it matter? For many reasons, but two stand out above the others. First, one out of every ten people in the world is malnourished. People are suffering; people are dying. It doesn't have to be that way, but unless the system is challenged and changed, it will continue to be. Second, it matters because our appropriation of benefits won at the cost of other people's hunger and suffering undermines our own well-being. We simply cannot be whole and happy while participating in a system that creates brokenness and misery for so many people.

Description: The costs of cheap food

How did it happen that what appears to be a good thing—relatively cheap food—is based on a system that causes hunger for many to the benefit of the well-off? This chapter examines the issue of food policy in the United States and other developed nations, especially the economics of food and the fact that one of the primary determinants of a successful food policy is low cost at the point of access, which for most people is the grocery store. Unless we understand that the U.S. cheap food policy is a field of systems that advantage some and disadvantage others, we will continue to feel a mix of emotions—basically satisfied with our food choices and their cost, sad that there are hungry people in the world, and quite overwhelmed by our personal inability to do much about it.

The hunger crisis impacting many countries in the world is due to a number of factors in affluent nations, including the subsidized diversion of grains into biofuels, global warming, and public policies that keep food prices low. If we understand (and increasingly we do) that our advantages come at the expense of others, we will reluctantly acquiesce to the "bargain" that is being conducted every day. We may concede to the status quo, but our consciences will not be clear, which is a good reason to join with others to challenge and change the system.

It is vital that we understand there is a high political price to be paid when costs at the checkout lines in American grocery stores are too high. This political fact of life can be illustrated by an incident from 1972. The price of food rose dramatically, in part because the Soviet Union purchased massive amounts of wheat and corn in what came to be known as the "great grain robbery." Higher grain prices meant higher grocery prices. As a matter of fact, nearly $54 billion was added to the food prices of American consumers between 1972 and 1975, the most rapid increase in a century. In March 1973, President Nixon responded to "housewives' demonstrations by putting a ceiling on red-meat prices, but by June, wholesale food prices still went up 19 percent above January."[1]

The message was clear. Politicians beware! The American consumer had become addicted to cheap food, and there were few sins less politically forgivable than high grocery prices. Thus, a cheap food policy, which had been widely touted before the great grain robbery, was reinforced. Governments topple when food prices rise precipitously.

Another thing that must be realized right up front is that food production in the United States and other affluent nations depends on oil. Food production and distribution are tied directly to this commodity, which is to say that food production and distribution have much to do with international relations, especially with oil-producing nations.

You noticed that I said there were "few sins less politically forgivable than high grocery prices." That has often been translated to suggest that the United States does indeed have a "cheap food policy"—and it appears to. Still, the following two propositions challenge that assumption.

Proposition 1: Cheap food isn't cheap

An example of the language justifying the success of the American food system states, "Government farm payments undoubtedly help farmers to stay in business, but they also benefit the entire population by helping to preserve our source of relatively inexpensive food. Currently only about 11 percent of our national disposable income is spent on food—the lowest of any developed nation."[2] Those percentages include both the costs of eating out and the costs of buying food and preparing meals at home. It is absolutely true that the U.S. consumer pays only 10 or 11 percent of their income for food; nevertheless, food in the United States is really not all that cheap.

If one analyzes what the percentages mean, they are really touting the nation's high median standard of living ($50,000). It is 10 or 11 percent of a high median income that represents the cost of food. So the Indian household that spends 51 percent of its $1,005 median income actually spends far less money on food ($513 vs. $4,223).[3] Thus, the claim about cheap food is really based on food affordability rather than absolute cost.

It should be noted, of course, that this discussion is looking at median income figures. If one has less than a median income, say a household with two children and a single mother earning less than a poverty-level income, then the percentage of income spent on food rises to 30 percent.

Industrial food is expensive in absolute terms and becoming more so, claim Drs. Salvador and Zdorkowski of Iowa State University. A unit of food that cost $1 seventy years ago now costs $38, and the Economic Research Service of the Department of Agriculture (ERS), a highly respected group, projects that per capita food expenditures will rise by another 7.1 percent over the next twenty years.[4] Rapid increases in food prices in the United States, and particularly in developing countries, however, suggest a far higher percentage.

The actual produce on average accounts for only 20 percent of the final retail cost of food. The U.S. citizen is paying for *ready access* to food, almost anywhere, anytime. Increasingly, however, social critics are asking whether this system is really as inexpensive as it is touted to be if one takes waste, health, environmental degradation, and overproduction into account.

Drs. Salvador and Zdorkowski put it bluntly: "The only reason we can actually afford such a questionable system is that we are so rich and so thoughtless about our food. Simple and sensible changes . . . could lead to major reductions in the health and ecological impacts of our food system, reduce our dependence on foreign oil, and directly benefit our farming sector."[5]

Another cost of the food system, which makes food so inexpensive at the checkout line, is the subsidy that the federal government gives to those who produce it. In 2005, farm subsidies were $23 billion, although other forms of support for farming, such as tariff protection from competing countries, added another $20 billion to the value of the government's support.[6] *U.S. News & World Report* suggests that these subsidies add $320 to the expenses of every man, woman, and child in the country.

Proposition 2: Cheap food comes at the expense of many others

It is instructive to explore exactly where those federal farm subsidies go. It is an illusion that subsidies put much money into the pockets of the family farmer. A full 80 percent of farm subsidies go to only 10 percent of the producers, many of them large-scale corporate operations. Many of those who benefit from the subsidy program live in New York City!

I was brought up to believe that we can equate the cost of a thing with its monetary price. The cheaper, the better—if the product is the same. And, in fact, the nation has fashioned a food policy that plays that tune. If one can get it cheaper, then that is better, at least on the face of it. But is it? Equating the cost of our food with what we pay disguises the real expense of the food. It allows us to remain somewhat unmindful of what it actually costs to bring food to our tables in terms of labor, fossil fuel consumption, and producers' living conditions. It is at this level that the issue of hunger and complicity begins. It is the reduction of food to its dollar-and-cents cost at the grocery store that disguises from us what food is, who we are, and what the parameters of our rights to food are. Behind the monetary price paid *for* food is what it *costs others* to produce, process, and distribute it.

Without going into too much detail, let me point out how the federal farm policy advantages some and disadvantages others. I have already indicated the political ramifications of high food prices. Federal farm policy, which once was designed to control the amount of corn, soybeans, rice, and wheat that was produced, has now been designed to ensure that there will be an abundance of basic commodities to eat. The federal farm program has paid farmers to produce regardless of its impact on the overall needs of the market. Farmers now regularly over-produce, and corporate farmers (and others, to the extent of their holdings) are subsidized. There is a minimal cap on the amount that large farms can gain from the federal subsidy ($1 million apiece for a married couple translates into a $2 million subsidy). This has put pressure on medium-sized operations to get bigger. As a result, some have grown and others have gotten out of the business entirely. Many others farm as a sideline—a "hobby" that produces only a small percentage of the total family income.

Sales taxes on food disadvantage the poor, and, as I have pointed out, a poor family pays a higher percentage of its income on food in the first place. So speaking of the *average* percentage of income spent on food masks the distribution of food costs and also hides the wastefulness, environmental costs, and amount of the national budget involved in the subsidization of the American food system.

At this point you might well ask, "How in the world can you say that we are complicit in this policy?" Perhaps the word *complicit* suggests a degree of guilt that is not intended. The word is one with many roots; one is *complice,* the Old French for "accomplice"; another is *complicem,* which means "partner or confederate." Those both imply more responsibility than I intend. Another meaning of the word *complicit* (which I am using) is from the Latin *complicare,* which means "to fold together," and/or "to complicate."[7] This meaning fits well with contemporary globalization—there are many folds or angles or plies to economic reality these days. Things are complicated, or folded together. We live in an era of complicity—weak complicity, perhaps, but one that is morally troubling. Our economic choices and behavior, when *folded in* to the larger economic system, often have far-reaching harmful consequences of which we may be largely unaware but that are nevertheless very real.

So what we are discussing is the degree of responsibility that Christians and others have to confront the complicated ways they come to appropriate (even unintentionally!) benefits that result from the miserable conditions and suffering of others. The act of appropriation is so pervasive and so enormously consequential that it is vital that we pay attention to it.

Let me emphasize that this is not simply one person's blindness or disease; if that were so, the problems would be easily remedied. This is instead a collective disease. It is written into the structures of our way of life. We could be immobilized by it, but that would result in hurting ourselves. And muting our concern because it is *not my problem* will only produce a muting of our compassion as well.

We will each go to hell reciting "not my problem." There is an analogy from the world of ecological concern—the phenomenon of global warming, whose perniciousness lies in the fact that people's present actions do not have presently visible and accountable consequences; instead, we are drawing on future earnings and will have to pay for present conveniences in a future where their negative impact is compounded. The devilish nature of appropriations is that the eventual costs of continuing to enjoy material abundance at the expense of others will be massive starvation and illness around the world. In this respect, one might note that the per capita income of many African countries has gone *down* in the past decade, and some reports suggest that U.S. per capita income is stagnant for lower income groups as well.

Besides the real-life consequences to people whose work is appropriated (starvation, HIV/AIDS, high probability of criminal victimization, and poor living conditions for self and children), those with a decent standard of living are blocked from a profound sense of well-being precisely by appropriating others' work and efforts. (I would not, of course, think of comparing the relative degrees of suffering.) Cheap food policies contribute to the appropriation of others' work and lives by the affluent. Many farmworkers are underpaid so we can afford to buy as much or more than we need to eat well. Migrant workers are kept in debt bondage, particularly when those workers are undocumented with no legal recourse to protect their workers' rights. Our restaurant bills are deflated by the low wages of servers, cooks, and busboys. The food we buy at the grocery store does not reflect the true cost of the labor to produce, process, and transport it and does not give a decent return to the producer. Even though prices are rising a bit, this appears to be a hiccup in a long-term trend and does not trickle down to higher wages for the poor.

It is simply true that major global corporations are realizing the benefits of our cheap food policy. It is not the medium-sized family farmer who realizes the benefits of cheap commodities; it is the Tysons, the Cargills, the ADMs, and their associates who benefit from cheap corn and soybeans and wheat. When one examines the percentages of the concentration of food business that is located in four or five major companies, the pattern becomes clear very quickly.

It should also be noted that we whose pensions are invested in companies holding shares of ConAgra and Cargill are sitting pretty. We might not condone the ways federal monies are diverted toward the already-wealthy, but we are largely silent because we benefit from it.

The implications of appropriation for happiness

We who have grown up in a materialist society, when confronted with the ways in which our comfortable lifestyles come at the expense of other people's having a decent living, often try to ignore the ways in which we are morally implicated. After all, to acknowledge complicity is to acknowledge a fundamental lack of well-being, an unhappiness, a spiritual malaise. We simply cannot be whole, we cannot enjoy well-being, unless we respond to the plight of others.

There are at least three basic responses to the realization of our complicity in the appropriation of others' lives and work: sharing, ignoring or avoiding, and justifying. The first response—sharing—recognizes and accepts the fact that many of the material benefits we enjoy have come through the contributions of others who live near or on the edge. Many individuals and organizations respond by sharing and do admirable work in alleviating hunger and suffering. Sharing emerges out of the desire to give back, to make living conditions better. There are many stories of people who exhibit this response; I will tell some of them later.

The second response—ignoring—is the effort not to recognize or accept the fact of appropriation and our complicity in it. By and large, this second response typifies those who *choose* to deny what is taking place. That is becoming increasingly difficult to do. Such avoidance or ignorance may be caused by a sense of being overwhelmed, but that does not excuse it.

The third response is an attempt to justify our personal good fortune. Those who seek to justify hunger and their complicity in it may feel as though they deserve what they have gotten through legal means. Those making this response simply accept their and others' situations as "fate" and consider the inequality of appropriation to be justifiable legally and morally.

Social scientists have been studying the question of happiness, and what they are finding is interesting. Perhaps the most-often-asked question in happiness studies is the age-old "Does money produce happiness?" The result is a mixed set of findings. Cross-cultural studies do find that people in countries where the median income is higher report a higher level of happiness. However, among affluent nations, such results cannot be explained as a direct correlation with wealth. Bruno Frey and Alois Stutzer report, in summary, that "income has a significant effect on happiness. People living in poor countries without any doubt become happier with increasing per capital income." But above the threshold of around U.S. $10,000, a higher average income no longer contributes much to subjective well-being, the most important reason being that people adjust their expectations to the rise in income.[8]

In terms of our three responses of sharing, ignoring, or justifying, the findings on happiness suggest that, beyond a certain minimum, having more does not bring happiness. We will later offer evidence that sharing in fact seems to be correlated with happiness more than the other two responses. Here, we are indicating the bare fact that happiness is not associated with the size of one's bank account or other holdings. Though we make jokes about it, we often live as though we could equate money with happiness. The fact is, we can't.

Before moving to a discussion of theological issues, let me tell a personal story that I suspect most of you can identify with to one degree or another. It is a story that illustrates how difficult it is to acknowledge the ways in which we are implicated in the suffering of others. It illustrates how easy it is to ignore, avoid, or justify. It is also a story that points to the possibility of reclaiming our shared humanity and well-being.

My morning route to Saint Paul School of Theology takes me past a QT gas station. The gas is a bit cheaper there and so I often stop. Early in the morning you can find quite a collection of people at the station. First, there are inevitably the police, who are sometimes talking to people and sometimes not. Then there are folks in beat-up old cars. There are blue-collar workers. There are any number of derelicts and people who look as though they have slept out in the open or not slept at all. Often there is an old woman whose shoes have seen much better days. This woman is gray-haired and wrinkled, and she often wears a worn gray sweatshirt and a nondescript skirt. She usually stands about five feet inside the door, looking as if she does not know where she is and certainly not where she is going.

I'll admit that I don't like seeing this woman, and I try to distance myself from her. She stands as a denial of the optimistic, upwardly mobile philosophy of Americanism and of some aspects of Christianity. She stands as a challenge to the "good life" and an indictment of the reality of appropriation. She makes me aware of my own vulnerability and insecurity. My temptation is to run from this person who exhibits vulnerability and pain.

I do not want to get in touch with that part of me that is her, that does not know where I am going and is wounded. I do not know her history. What sort of housing can she afford? What does she eat? Does she have a job? Does it have benefits? And how does her experience benefit me? She threatens my sense of well-being. But she is also the possibility of relationship and renewed well-being. But to realize that possibility, as we will see, will take faith and courage and a coming together with others to end the injustices of our system in the name of our shared humanity.

It seems that there is little delight in that woman's life, nor does she share in the abundance many of us take for granted. In the research for my book *Food for Life: The Spirituality and Ethics of Eating*, I discovered that the biblical witness suggests that God has two purposes for eating: delight and sharing. That is, God desires that every person and indeed every creature—no exceptions—enjoy their eating and delight in it. Furthermore, as made clear through the example of both the Old Testament prophets and Jesus, God desires that every person share their food with others. God's policy is not a cheap food policy.

We should note, of course, that this is not simply a Christian concern. All of the major religions hold that it is essential that people care for each other and the planet. Hunger and its alleviation are a concern for people of faith across the spectrum of religions.[9] Indeed, people of different faith traditions ought to be talking to and working with each other to make it happen.

Theological perspective: A theology of grace for appropriation

The question "Why is appropriation a morally troublesome category?" is a decidedly religious question for people of faith. Remember, "appropriation" is our shorthand for labeling a person's or group's or even a nation's obtaining benefits at the cost of other people's suffering. If our faith compels us to believe that we should care for each other and all life, then the fact of appropriation is indeed morally and spiritually troublesome.[10]

What is it in a person's formation that leads him or her to be concerned about appropriation? I will address this question from the perspective of Christian faith, although it should be noted that people of other faiths or of no faith may share these core beliefs, even if they might formulate them differently.

When Christians think theologically about the contradiction between abundance and hunger, we begin with the notion that God loves us and gives us everything we need and much that we simply want. God gives. The grace of God is such that, like a loving parent, God absolutely adores us and gives unconditionally. God loves God's creation. The nature of God is overflowing abundance lavished on us without measure. God gives and gives and gives. As theologian Kathryn Tanner put it:

> God is always offering the whole of the good to everyone, limited only by our capacities to receive, limitations that may be the product of natural forms of finitude or of a divinely arranged diversity of roles in church or society, but are more likely the result of our own sinful institution of contrary, competitive economies.[11]

John Calvin made the sovereignty of God's grace the cornerstone of his theology. Martin Luther used the image of an overflowing fountain showering gifts on all God's creatures to describe God's grace. The unconditional giving of God is evident in the abundance of creation.

God gives with no thought as to what might be received in return. That is the nature of God's giving. As Tanner put it, "The priority is extending benefits. That is what unconditional giving is all about, after all: an extension of benefits beyond the usual conditions that are placed on them in loans and sales."[12] The nature of God's grace implies that human social relations should not be based on merit or anticipated returns. God gives without the characteristics of the receiver influencing the gift. As Jesus said, God "makes his sun rise on the evil and on the good, and sends rain on the righteous and on the unrighteous" (Matt. 5:45). Thus, all are given both the gifts of creation and continuing regard.

Furthermore, God continues to gift creatures, no matter what they do in return. It is human sinfulness that interrupts the gift, in fact refusing to receive it. It is not God who has stopped giving; rather it is we who have stopped receiving. This is a real loss to us, both because we cannot enjoy God's gifts and because it is to our detriment that we do not receive them. The most pernicious consequence of sin is what it does to us, the damage that it does to who we are.

When we set the divine economy alongside the cheap food policy, we see that they are in opposition. God's is an abundant, gratuitous, and scrumptious food policy—a great banquet. The prophet Isaiah pictures Yahweh beckoning his hearers:

Ho, everyone who thirsts,
    come to the waters;
and you that have no money,
    come, buy and eat!
Come, buy wine and milk,
    without money and without price.
Why do you spend your money for that which is not
        bread,
    and your labor for that which does not satisfy?
Listen carefully to me, and eat what is good,
    and delight yourselves in rich food. (Isa. 55:1-2)

God is the consummate giver, loving unconditionally and not requiring or demanding or compelling any return gift. The contrast between this and the cheap food policy becomes crystal clear when one asks, "Who gets to eat?" The cheap food policy answers, "Those who have the money." The divine economy answers, "All God's creatures, for free." Obviously that is not the way the world works, but it is what we should strive for.

The claim that God gives unconditionally to all may seem to bear little resemblance to the way the world is; it is easy to dismiss it as an ideal that has little connection to empirical reality—a lovely thought, but no more than a dream of the way things should be. All should have abundance, but abundance is a dream, right? Wrong.

Abundance is real, but our blindness, finitude, and sin prevent us from recognizing, accepting, and living this reality. With respect to God's abundance, we make a critical mistake if we believe that God gives *directly* to individuals. God's unconditional giving is not found in direct divine handouts; it is found in the incredible fecundity of creation. There is enough for all to have enough. It is the way God created the world. The problem is not a lack of abundance; it is with human systems that grant access to abundance to some while denying access to others. Once again, the system of appropriation whereby some benefit at the expense of others rears its ugly head and distorts the divine economy.

And yet the claim that God continuously gives to all through the fruitfulness of creation, along with the claim that men and women have been created in the image of God (Gen. 1:26-29), suggests that it is within our capacity to live in such a way that equal access to abundance becomes more and more a human reality. It is not a pipe dream; there are many examples of men and women, singly and in groups, who are living in the reality of abundance for all. The intention of God that all delight in God's abundant provision offers us a different understanding of the world and of our relationship with other people and creatures as a whole than the understanding of the world embodied in current economic and food policies. That is truly exciting.

Moral directions: Improving the problem of appropriation with a new vision

Several times I have called the issue of our cheap food policy morally troublesome or even sinful. Globalization, which contributes to the strength of the cheap food policy, has thrust humankind into a situation where new realities have stretched our moral vocabulary thin or even broken the elasticity of the terms. Globalization is so diffuse that it is difficult (and incorrect) to pin responsibility on any one person or group of persons. What makes the cheap food policy problematic is that each person contributes to its persistence in such slight (and mentally displaceable) ways that it is easy to fall into ignoring or justifying its existence. Nevertheless, from the perspective of God's economy, the cheap food economy clearly constitutes a misappropriation and can be judged immoral.

I invite you to think with me about new directions based on the vision that we began to articulate above. Castigating certain organizations, groups, or individuals does not offer a pathway toward ameliorating this problem of appropriation. Rather, let us begin by asking what the economy or reign of God commends.

First, we can affirm, based on the belief that God continually gives to all creatures through the fruitfulness of creation, that God wills the good for *all* life. God imbues all of creation with God's goodness and yearns for us to flourish with the whole family of life. This is at the heart of the Christian message. The Reformed tradition ties the sovereignty of God with God's perfect love; the Roman Catholic tradition speaks of the sacramental principle whereby God shines forth in all reality, mediating the love of God to us. Episcopalian John Koenig reminds us that God indwells our meals and is present in the world we inhabit.[13] In multiple ways different Christian traditions all maintain that the will of God for the good of all is the bedrock affirmation of their faith. It is also the foundation of Christian morality.

On the principle that God wills the good for all life, we can say that God desires that we enjoy our lives. Those material things that make for enjoyment of life are good. Enjoyment is good. God wills that we enjoy abundance. The world was created, in part, for our enjoyment and for the enjoyment of all creatures. The material world is not evil, nor is it wrong to enjoy ourselves. God wants us to flourish, to live as satisfying and happy a life as possible. In fact, that is the way God planned it. God wants all creatures to delight in the goodness of creation. A social, political, or economic order that inhibits such enjoyment for all runs counter to God's will and can be judged immoral.

Cheap food policies as currently established are constructed so as to guarantee low cost to some at the expense of others; producers seek competitive advantages, whether by hiring migrant workers or growing in locales where wages are low. Social policies built on such competitiveness tend to perpetuate social privilege and disadvantage those who have not had the chance to develop or enjoy their capabilities. Which is to say they violate God's vision of equal access to abundance and a good life for everyone—no exceptions—and can be judged immoral. Indeed, Kathryn Tanner shows that contrasting policies built on interdependence have the advantage of being more sustainable in the long run.[14]

From a Christian moral perspective, there is considerable pressure to ensure that everyone enjoys the benefits of food that is abundant, good, safe, accessible, and nutritious and that arrives at our tables with justice for the producer. Furthermore,

if this moral goal were achieved, it would add to our own pleasure in eating. We could know that the food we eat is both good
and just.

Steps toward transformation

The moral direction in which our faith perspective points is
that of promoting full enjoyment, of being able to receive what
God gives. The image is of our being so profoundly joy-full that
we are eager to share. The complicity of appropriating benefits
that come at the expense of others would become repugnant to
us, even repulsive. We would know that our own well-being
is compromised by the other's suffering at our expense. Mal-
nourishment, to say nothing of starvation, in a world of plenty
would become morally heinous to us.

We know, however, that we are a long way from realizing
such an ideal distribution. How might we learn that giving is
not that far from receiving? How might we learn that the well-
being of others is, at least ultimately if not immediately, my
well-being and certainly the well-being of the earth community? What steps might make for transformation, particularly
with respect to the cheap food policy? How can we begin to
undo complicity in this area? The power of this policy is finally
couched in the myth that "cheaper is better."[15] Following are
ways in which we might start to demythologize that idea and
begin to undo our complicity.

Raise awareness

Reversing complicity begins by becoming aware of the ways
in which we have been socialized as consumers or shoppers.
We have cut our teeth on searching for bargains, and whatever

media we attend to reinforces the value of "the bargain." Thus, we tend to equate the value of a standardized product (if it is not a luxury item) with price. A tomato is a tomato is a tomato, right? Wrong! We are becoming aware that what goes into a product is far more than price. We are beginning to discover the difference between a "gas-fired tomato" that has traveled 1,300 miles and one that was picked yesterday a few miles away. If you need further persuading on this score, read author Barbara Kingsolver's work on the joys of tomatoes.[16] We are slowly recognizing that the same price covers many differences.

Global economics too often promotes a "race to the bottom"; whoever can deliver a product most cheaply wins—no matter the wages paid, the illness engendered, the family life disrupted, the hunger increased, or—within bounds—the quality of the product. The word of hope in this situation is that more and more people are becoming aware of the true cost of food. The price we pay does not represent the total expense of the bread or meat we eat. The first step toward reversing complicity is becoming aware of it; the anti-sweatshop movement has many parallels in the food industry.

Make confession

For people of faith, undoing complicity will involve confessing before God that we sometimes put price before relationship. As we become aware of the inequity in the system, even though we neither intend nor desire to perpetuate it, we realize that we are part of it. As a matter of fact, it is God's grace and our awareness of God's forgivingness, alongside our complicity, that enables us to be aware of and repent of our role in appropriating cheap food and other benefits. Knowing that we can be forgiven and enter into a closer relationship with God enables us to repent and begin to reverse our participation in sinfulness. As we come closer to God, we come closer to our neighbor. We see that God desires that we care for the neighbor as much as we care for ourselves. This is after all the second great commandment (Lev. 19:18; Matt. 22:39; Mark 12:33; Luke 10:27). The cheap prices we pay violate our neighbor's well-being, and such injustice is not God's way. Nor does it foster our own well-being. We are to give as well as receive, to put a concern for the lives of others above our consumer concerns. Transformation requires that we repent and confess to God what has become obvious to us—our complicity.

Accept forgiveness

Forgiveness can lead to transformation. It is a relief to confess before God because such self awareness and penance free us to accept God's forgiveness with gratitude. It allows us to acknowledge the truth that has taken a lot of energy to disguise—the truth of our complicity. Repentance and confession are the foundation of transformation. In Christian theological terms, justification enables us to move toward sanctification. Freed from entrapment in cheap prices, we are enabled to love the neighbor as much if not more than our bank accounts or gourmet eating habits. We may well find renewed and redeemed relationships with our neighbors more satisfying than cheap prices.

There are more concrete steps toward transformation. Sometimes we act in new ways of thinking, and this may be especially the case when we confront such entrenched habits as shopping for the lowest prices (in terms of dollars and cents). The following are suggestions that can help us move away from cheap-but-unjust food policies:

1. We could enlarge our sense of what enters into a price. What does that fast food meal cost in terms of nutrition, relationships, and satisfaction? What all is entailed in our eating besides the dollars and cents? And with cheap food, are we getting our money's worth? All these factors enter into the price of a rib eye or artichokes: fertilizer, cheap labor, environmental factors, fossil fuel emissions, antibiotics, and pesticides. Who pays those aspects of the price? My suggestion here is simply that we become aware of what enters into the price of a product beyond the $6.79 a pound we spend for it at the checkout. We have long known about the effect of externalizing environmental factors, but do we also externalize factors such as our own health and well-being? The suggestion here is that we stretch the meaning of "price" to include a wider range of factors.

2. We can learn where our food comes from and how it gets to our tables. Who are we paying when we buy at a national chain store, a local grocery, a farmers' market, or a community-supported agricultural farm (CSA) or when we harvest from our own backyard gardens? What sort of wages does my grocery store pay its workers, and how does it keep prices so low? Where is the food being grown? By whom? At what cost?

All these factors enter into price. There is a Hundred Mile Diet Club whose members seek to eat produce that is grown within that radius. One question that often arises is how prices at farmers' markets compare to those offered by supermarkets or grocery stores. While there is little current research, two older, rigorous studies give the price advantage to farmers' markets. In terms of taste, community support, and environmental impact, there is no contest.[17] Another factor is that buyers' money tends to stay "closer to the ground" and "closer to home," benefiting their communities. This locavore (local food) movement has many advocates. For our purposes, spending for local produce tends to result in more equitable payment of farmers and laborers.

3. A similar international movement—fair trade efforts—seeks to compensate local growers at a higher rate than the open market would. To be sure, this will not eradicate the complicity of appropriation, but it is important to do what we can rather than be overwhelmed by global economic forces. And what we can do can be pretty impressive. If every food-buying household in our country were to spend $15 of its weekly grocery allocation on local or fairly traded food, it would represent an enormous accomplishment. There are, conservatively, 100 million "buying units" in this country (300 million people divided by 2.57 persons per household). Fifteen dollars a week spent with fair trade vendors, farmers' markets, community-supported farms, or other local direct sales outlets represents the buying power of $1.5 billion *weekly*, or $78 billion a year. That amount of spending could begin to break the connection between cheap food and cheap labor. It could lead to a notion of moral parity. And we would feel good about it!

4. Politics matters economically. The fact is that poor nations subsidize rich ones. According to *New York Times Magazine* journalist Tina Rosenberg, "Everyone in a wealthy nation has become the beneficiary of the generous subsidies that poorer countries bestow upon rich ones."[18] With the advent of globalized markets and "free" trade agreements, capital began to move from South to North. The South now exports capital to the North, according to the United Nations. In 2006, the net transfer of capital from poorer to rich countries was $784 billion. In 2002, it was $229 billion. In 1997, the balance was even.[19] It is a disturbing trend. Meeting the World Trade Organization's requirements have added costs to countries in the South, as have subsidies, patents, and copyrights—including

pharmaceuticals—and the tax benefits offered to corporations. According to Rosenberg, "Sometimes reverse subsidies are disguised. Rich-country governments spent $283 billion in 2005 to support and subsidize their own agriculture, mainly agribusiness. Artificially cheap food exported to poor countries might seem like a gift, but it is actually a Trojan horse."[20] The local food economy of poorer nations is thereby undercut. How can we feel good about cheap food when it comes at such a high cost? We simply have to attend to federal and international policies that benefit us inequitably and disproportionately. We need to begin to support policies and practice buying habits that will represent a just food policy, one that we can feel has contributed to others' being well fed.

5. We do have any number of allies in this effort. Bread for the World is an organization that monitors food systems all over the globe and advocates for just food policies, especially for those countries where hunger is rampant. Their grassroots lobbying efforts over the years have made a great difference in this fight. There are organizations such as the Foods Resource Bank that work to support international hunger and development work around the world. There are also organizations such as Oxfam, Second Harvest, and Heifer International that seek to redress the injustices of the global food system. Most denominations have hunger programs that are active in working to relieve hunger. Much is being done that deserves our understanding, participation, and support.

Questions for digestion

1. We in the United States may complain about food prices going up. We may even feel that our food is no longer cheap. What is going on psychologically when we do

that? Is that a way of avoiding a sense of complicity or denying that we are benefiting? Why or why not?

2. Maybe the term "cheap food" is a misnomer or just flat wrong. Who or what pays the price for cheap food? We probably cannot point to any one person as the cause of this suffering. Does this make our food crisis a more or less significant moral issue?

3. According to theologian Kathryn Tanner, "God is always offering the whole of the good to everyone." Why do you think that seems difficult to believe? What happens if we believe that God will continue to give, no matter what our response is?

4. What concrete social policies would be changed if our primary moral goal was to "promote full enjoyment for everyone"? What would that mean about the way the system distributed food?

5. Can you imagine two ways we could begin to reverse complicity?

2

Healthy Food,
Healthy Humans

Garrett Hardin, a biologist renowned for his metaphor of "Life-boat Earth," said something at a Food, Farming, and the Future symposium that I will never forget.

Hardin said, "You can never do only one thing." By that, of course, he meant that the world is interconnected, every part to every part.

I can't say that I remember that every time I visit the Burger King drive-thru and get a Whopper. (Hold the cheese, I'm a healthy eater, right?) As I drive along with a burger in one hand and the other on the wheel, the pleasure is momentary. About five minutes later my stomach feels like someone dropped a sack of marbles in it. What my mind perceived as a fast meal, my stomach perceived as a mass of fat and cholesterol. They are connected. The Immokalee workers whom we met earlier may have picked some of those Burger King tomatoes. They may have grown the corn that fed the beef that became my Whopper. You can never do only one thing.

Description: High costs to health

I don't need to tell you that one of the prices of cheap food is our health. This whole sector of the food system is evidenced by "too much." If you don't believe me, just go to a mall and sit in one place (maybe the food court?) for about forty-five minutes and observe the people passing by. We are fat. Now, I know fat, and I hate my fat. And it seems to me that while we contribute to our own bad health, there are other culprits besides ourselves who are responsible.

In order to keep food cheap, U.S. policy has encouraged the growing of too much of it. As a matter of fact, we produce 3,900 calories of food per day for every man, woman, and child in this country. The average intake of calories has increased by about 10 percent since 1977. That increase is concurrent with a food policy dedicated to the overproduction of grain. "Since that time," writes author Michael Pollan, "farmers in the United States have managed to produce 500 additional calories per person every day. Each of us is, heroically, managing to pack away about 200 of those extra calories per day. Presumably the other 300—most of them in the form of surplus corn—get dumped on overseas markets or turned into ethanol."[1]

There is ample documentation that we are indeed a fat food nation. One of the most alarming statistics is the rise in type 2 diabetes among children. Type 2 diabetes used to be confined to adults, but all that high fructose corn syrup had to go somewhere. The super-sizing of soft drinks and candy has contributed its share as well.

Pollan makes a remarkable claim about our food industry: the industry itself, nutritional science, and journalism all have "like a large gray fog" generated "a great Conspiracy of Confusion" that has gathered around the simplest questions of nutrition—"much to the advantage of everyone involved. Except perhaps the ostensible beneficiary of all this nutritional expertise and advice: us, and our health and happiness as eaters."[2]

Pollan's story takes as one of its defining moments the issuing in 1977 of a report on "Dietary Goals for the United States." The report observed that during the years of World War II, "when meat and dairy products were strictly rationed, the rate of heart disease temporarily plummeted. . . . Henceforth, government dietary guidelines would shun talk about whole foods, each of which has its trade association on Capitol Hill, and would instead arrive clothed in scientific euphemism and speaking of nutrients, entities that few Americans really understood but that lack powerful lobbies in Washington."[3] What we do know is that people who eat an American diet tend to die of cancer, heart disease, diabetes, and obesity.

It would be too easy to foist off our responsibility onto the commodity lobbyists or Big Food. Though they play their part, we are increasingly learning what we are doing to ourselves. The bad news is that we are all complicit in this. The bag of lettuce that is so convenient to use travels many miles and has a certain amount of farmworker labor tied up in it. The box of cereal requires a quarter gallon of gasoline to be brought to our table. Our tax money funds the $19 billion subsidy (2005) that Big Food enjoys. We vote with our dollars and support the system that is bringing us ill health. The United States' national ill health is consuming more and more of our national budget as well.

One of the most reliable predictors of obesity and poor health is poverty. Poor people eat cheap, bad food. There is of course nothing wrong with enabling the hungry (often the poor) to eat by selling food cheaply. There is nothing wrong with a healthy diet or food that the poor can afford. Indeed, producing affordable healthy food is admirable. However, our food policies are more driven by economic incentives than by the health of consumers. We do not eat a diet that is healthy, and we should be outraged about that—for ourselves, our children, and those who are ill treated by the production of foods that are not even healthy for we who appropriate them. For example, we subsidize foods that are unhealthy for us and fail to subsidize the vegetables and fruits that are the heart of good health. Why is that?

Speaking at the second Terra Madre conference in 2004, England's Prince Charles reminded his audience that it was not only the poor and not only those in the two-thirds world who were susceptible to the disease of poor nutrition: "There is now a growing body of evidence that suggests that in the so-called developed world we are in the process of creating a nutritionally impoverished underclass—a generation which has grown up on highly processed fast food from intensive agriculture and for whom the future looks particularly bleak, both from a social and health perspective."[4]

There is a false perception that health is a "purely" physical matter and that it is an individual one. It is neither. Health is also a cultural and spiritual matter. Eating is a spiritual discipline in which we honor our bodies. Exercise, proper diet, sleep, and all that goes into respecting the limits and capabilities of our bodies are forms of self-care and also a way of discipleship—part of our relationship with God. Christian and various other religious traditions have taught that what goes into a person weighs significantly in what comes out. Nutritional educator and author Deborah Kesten found that "in addition to the Hindu belief that espouses approaching food with loving regard, other wisdom traditions encourage us to honor food, and to partake of it with a depth and sincerity that makes it sacred. . . . The implication: when we furnish food with such sacred understanding, it will nourish both body and soul in ways that we have been depriving ourselves of."⁵

Certainly the values of a Christian understanding that the "body is a temple of the Holy Spirit" (1 Cor. 6:19) and the culture's quest for the fit, dynamic, and voluptuous body can seem to be consistent. One way of "honoring the body" is by taking care of it. Sometimes, of course, this can become an idolatrous habit, as demonstrated by books such as *The God of Thinness* by Mary Louise Bringle (Abingdon, 1992) and *Starving for Salvation* by Michelle Lelwica (Oxford, 2002). Looking at the issue from a different perspective, Harvard Divinity School professor Stephanie Paulsell's book *Honoring the Body* presents a well-balanced and fairly comprehensive consideration of the role of this practice in the Christian life.⁶

The value of consumption is accompanied by the value of control. It is fascinating to me that the very affluent are rarely obese or even overweight. A beautiful or handsome appearance is part of the glamour of being wealthy. The very affluent apparently have achieved the capacity to consume in huge quantities but also to control their weight; they have the means to maintain svelte figures. That would seem to be the ideal in our country. It is also part of our consumer lifestyle. We are obsessed with both consuming and being in control. We are, frankly, obsessed with—among other things—eating correctly. We want to control, to sculpt, our bodies. (Doesn't that sound great? "Sculpting" your body? Note the combination of control and beauty.)

The implications of appropriation for happiness

How is it that our lack of health is an issue of complicity or appropriation? I believe that this is an area where our misappropriation and the suffering of others are joined most solidly. We appropriate the good food that comes to us through low wages and misuse of land in distant nations whose cost is subsidized by our government, but we find that the corn fructose and red meat and fat and sugars are squeezing our arteries. That is, our complicity in the hunger and malnutrition of others is joined to our own overconsumption and malnutrition. There is, in short, such a thing as "too much of a good thing," and it is biting us in the stomach and in the *gluteus maximus* and in our hearts. The lack of balance and equity in our complicity, however unconscious and however unfair, is doing us in. The poor health resulting from too much that we don't enjoy comes at the cost of many others' poor health that comes from not enough.

Our high-powered economy is based on growth, but some of that growth is not what we want. We have a hard time climbing stairs or walking. I believe that this collective obesity is contributing to our lack of well-being. The idea that more is better no longer matches reality. In fact, once our basic needs are met, the very opposite seems to be the case. Once measured to have the happiest citizens in the developed world, the United States now ranks twenty-third, according to research compiled at the University of Leicester. Alcoholism, suicide, and depression rates have soared, with fewer than one in three Americans claiming to be "very happy." Even more frightening is the trickle-down effect of this malaise on our kids. Studies suggest that today's average American child reports suffering higher levels of anxiety than the average child under psychiatric care in the 1950s.[7]

Several factors seem to contribute to our overweight and our unhappiness. First, it seems fairly obvious that being overweight is not healthy and, to some extent, contributes negatively to happiness. Does that mean that you cannot be mentally healthy and overweight? No, but it certainly takes more work.

A second factor is the increasing isolation that often accompanies being overweight. Overweight kids tend to be those who watch the most television, an activity often done in isolation, and those with eating disorders often distance themselves from others, binging and purging in secret. A third factor that seems to be increasing is the "bowling alone" phenomenon—that is, there are fewer people with whom we share community. If one measures community as "those with whom one can share almost anything," then a 2006 report indicates that the average number of people with whom one shares intimate community has dropped from three to two in the past decade.

Theological perspective: The economy of God's grace

If the very nature of God is to be a giving and loving God, then the second facet of God's nature—almost indistinguishable from the first—is that God wills the best for all. God gives to all. God's delight is that we all flourish. God's will is that we all be healthy and live in the way that God created us to live, by delighting in the good things of this world and by sharing with all. Closely connected to the love of God is the second affirmation: God wills to have communion with and among all living beings. The world was created in *shalom*, designed so that all life might flourish. We do not flourish alone but in communion with one another, in community. That is what an individualistic understanding of health does not comprehend. We are relational beings, and our spiritual wholeness is not reducible to physical wellness. Christians celebrate Holy Communion, the Lord's Supper, Eucharist, to signify that we are the body of Christ, the God-man who took on flesh and became the body of creation to gather all beings into himself.

We have an image of what it means for God to will that all people have sufficient material goods and health to enjoy their lives. Jesus aligned himself with fishermen, tax collectors, and all manner of people. These disreputable or barely reputable people had no more and no less standing in God's community than those who were the most respected or the healthiest. There is a remarkable emphasis on physical health in the Gospels. It becomes clear that Jesus saw illness as an immediate concern. He did not wait until the Sabbath was over to heal the sick. The stories of his miracles center around restoring to wholeness those who were lame or crippled or suffered from leprosy, and Jesus sent the disciples out to do the same. God's love is unconditional and universal, and we are to use this economy of grace as a model to fashion our little economies, our health care system, and the way we distribute goods.

The reason inequalities exist and some people are more "fortunate" than others may be attributed to accidents of birth or to our system of competitive economics—or perhaps to the way sin is transmitted socioeconomically. If we were to live a healthy, God-intended, God-bearing lifestyle, then there would be (or could be) more for those whose health is compromised by too little food, too little vaccine, too little health care. We are called to imitate God's economy of grace and Jesus' concern for the health care of all people. We are called to strive in our laws, customs, and norms to promote actions that emulate the ideal standard of God's reign.

An important question that this understanding of God's inclusiveness raises is "What are the bounds of our community?" The Greek word *oikos* means "household." The question that cultural historian Thomas Berry puts to us is this: "What are the bounds of our household, our *oikos*? More and more it is clear that the bounds of our household are the entire planet.

If we consider the planet our *oikos*, then it is much easier to see why it is that other's well-being depends on us, and ours on others."[8] God would have us live in light of the whole species and earth being our *oikos*. Not that so living will continue the benefits God offers, or that not living that way will stop them, but only so as to be what God intends us fully to be, that is, to flourish alongside all life. We respond to God's giving by giving ourselves. We do not have to give; we want to give, because we know that giving and receiving are God's design. Living in that way will lead to profound well-being.

Moral directions

The moral norm governing health care that flows from God's intention that all life should flourish is that of distributive justice. The inclusiveness of God's love entails the norm that human beings should care for each other's well-being. The interdependence that characterizes globalization teaches us that our well-being depends on others and that, material accumulation aside, being able to appreciate one's life depends on others' being able to enjoy theirs. Systems should be designed to foster continually greater degrees of inclusiveness and health.

Social policies built on competitiveness tend to perpetuate social privilege and distribute health care to those who can afford it. Competitive policies disadvantage those who have not had the chance to develop or enjoy their capabilities. Indeed, theologian Kathryn Tanner shows that policies built on interdependence (and many are) have the advantage of being more sustainable in the long term.[9]

Justice is the norm that expresses the value of equity in relations, or fairness. Equals should be treated equally. Within the theological framework we are appealing to, all persons are equal. (The issue of how animals, plants, and abiotic beings are to be treated is a significant issue that will receive brief attention later.) Justice is the norm that expresses what we "owe" each other. This can be broken down into several aspects: contributive justice, sustainable justice/development, restorative justice, and distributive justice.

Distributive justice is the norm that applies to health care in this context. How should the good things of this life, including especially health care and food, be distributed? The notion of "owing" others is one way distributive justice has been expressed; that sort of language suggests a condescension on the part of the affluent or a notion that we deserve what we have and our obligation to others is minimal. That is hardly a connotation of distributive justice consistent with a God of grace who loves all his beings. Distributive justice expresses our relationship with others; it recognizes that we are all thrown into different situations with different life-chances and that your well-being contributes to mine and mine to yours. Thus, it will be better—it will contribute to the common good—if you do well and so do I. Corporately we will flourish if the basic goods of life are distributed in a basic sufficiency.

Thus, distributive justice commends a minimal level of material goods for all. This level should guarantee that everyone be able to have a decent life, with necessary food, shelter, health, and safety. Note that I am claiming this will be the best situation for all of us. I recognize that this is the minimum, the starting point. How opportunities, education, and assets get distributed after this guaranteed minimum is a matter, again, of the common good. The economy of grace is a noncompetitive one, and there are already "hooks" in our capitalist system, which is built on cooperation. These features enable the society to maintain a basic noncompetitive equilibrium. In the future it will become even more important to ensure that all parts of the global economic system are functioning synergistically in a way to promote the relative well-being of all. Should this mean that we the affluent have to forgo luxuries, so be it. We could well find that the healthy functioning of the whole system makes for our overall happiness.

There have been a number of food-related scares in the past decade: mad cow disease, hoof-and-mouth epidemic, E. coli scares, meat recalls, avian flu, and salmonella-tainted peanut butter—the list could go on and on. More and more our global food supply system makes for safe food and healthy food—or not. The interconnection of the system means that we cannot be sure of the source of the food. The connection between food safety, human health, and our appropriation of global food means that the world as a whole needs to find a way to ensure the health and well-being of all, or at least to take obvious steps in that direction. It is difficult to know how seriously to take the report that our food and water supplies are subject to bioterrorism, but we do know that working to improve human health is enormously satisfying. And there is progress here; the Carter Center's virtual eradication of the guinea worm is encouraging.

Steps toward transformation

We quite simply have a problem with health care in the United States. The basic problem is that we eat too much and that—alongside food that is too fatty and sugar-filled and carbohydrate-rich—we have adopted a lifestyle of overconsumption. We need to look after our own health. It really is a mystery how, in a country that is so wealthy and has such great medical research facilities, so many of us are overweight and even obese. And that obesity has not rendered us very happy. As a matter of fact, the obsessive attention we pay to our diet and the amount of money we spend on liposuction and weight-loss programs and diet regimes seem to be having exactly the opposite effect. We want a way to do this without discipline and in the face of having exquisite and wonderful foods. We want our cake without calories.

There is another side to this as well. (Isn't there always!) We operate with an interventionist rather than preventive model of health care, and we think of health as being solely an individual matter (nonrelational). Our system is geared to kick in when someone is sick or hurt rather than to promote health and well-being by eating and living well. We very much need to stop living so high on the hog, both for our own sake and for the sake of those who have too little.

You know the rules:

1. Eat mainly plant-based foods.
2. Limit your intake of red meats.
3. Use alcohol in moderation.
4. Your diet shouldn't be more than 15 percent fats.
5. Exercise regularly.
6. Get eight hours of sleep.

These are mundane things a person can do daily to improve her or his health. Many people in the United States and other high-consumption countries would benefit from consuming less. That is so obvious as almost to make me angry. It is not easy to consume less if every media surrounding us encourages us to consume more. One concern of this book is that we learn to consume ethically. However, consuming ethically is not the same as simply consuming less. What we need is to develop a way of simplifying our lives that is attractive, engaging, and fulfilling.

Religious groups are well positioned to help adherents reflect on their lifestyles and consider whether they would be better off by living more simply. The move toward simplifying one's life and consuming less will almost undoubtedly be a step in the direction of greater health, since most of our health problems arise from too much food, too much fat, too much stress, and too much anxiety. We are becoming more aware of the primacy of lifestyle issues to the anti-hunger movement. It is clear, moreover, that legislators won't act until we the citizens do.

Furthermore, it is amazing how unanimous the world's religions are in support of balanced consumption. The Baha'i faith counsels that "moderation in all things is desirable," warning that carrying things to excess will produce evil. Buddhism warns against craving and sees calmness coming to those who abandon selfish craving. Jesus taught that it is impossible to try to serve both God and wealth (Matt. 6:24) The Qur'an, 7:31, offers this wisdom: "Eat and drink, but waste not by excess: He loves not the excessive." Confucianism, Hinduism, Daoism, and Judaism have similar perspectives. The health benefits of Levitical dietary laws have often been commended.

We also can learn from the truly inspiring stories of individual men and women who have spearheaded medical advances. Author Tracy Kidder in the book *Mountain beyond Mountains* tells the story of Dr. Paul Farmer and his heroic efforts in Haiti to set up clinics, train medical practitioners, and fight HIV/AIDS.[10] Farmer recently has extended his work to Rwanda.

There are far-less-well-known, everyday people who are courageously involved in AIDS/HIV work around the world. One of those is Tsepang Setaka, a twenty-three-year old woman living with AIDS in Lesotho, a township in South Africa. Setaka is an "expert patient"—a local citizen who visits all the villages in areas so remote that one can get there only by foot or on the back of a horse or donkey. As an expert patient, she combats the stigma and fear of AIDS and tries to convince others to be tested so that they can get proper care and treatment.

There could well be a place for the use of "expert patients" (patients who have experienced the disease firsthand) in affluent countries, especially among those in poverty. We mistakenly assume that lower-income or even affluent people have the knowledge and the ability to take care of themselves in regard to their eating habits, hygiene, sleep, and nutrition, in particular. However, as the figures show, this is not always the case. It may be that national efforts to combat obesity should reconsider farm policies that produce low prices for food that is fatty or high in carbohydrates. There are of course other culprits—among them, excessive alcohol consumption, too much red meat, too little exercise, and not enough sleep. Perhaps our nation's nutritionists could find a way both to make use of "expert patients" and to turn the weight-loss industry into a public service entrepreneurial project. There is an educational, a psychological, a social, and a spiritual element to this. The finding that people who are overweight tend to have overweight friends suggests that a group approach to becoming healthier might bear fruit. It could be a way of addressing obesity and eating disorders across income groups, and a way that could work well in a church group setting.

Our conception of holistic health is one that many who work with children in poverty know firsthand. From the perspective of a doctor, it makes no sense for a hospital to discharge a poor child back to the slums without following up. But that is the norm for many children, and Dr. Vera Cordeiro of Brazil intends to change that. "To her, health and social conditions are two sides of the same coin. 'Hospital treatment as it is conducted today—ignoring poverty and the conditions of the family—is a *false* treatment,' she explains."[11] The same understanding of health as a holistic matter or condition has led human rights advocate Jeroo Billimoria of India to institute Childline, a telephone answering service for children who need referral or protection. Run by children trained by Jeroo and her team, children may call Childline for health reasons or for other conditions. This understanding of health as a holistic life status is one that we in the United States and other "developed nations" would do well to emulate.

There are domestic social entrepreneurs to whom we are indebted for better health as well. Dr. Edward Freis's discoveries about blood pressure and hypertension had been languishing for four years when American health activist and philanthropist Mary Woodward Lasker learned about his discovery of a drug that offered significant protection for moderate or severe hypertension. Thanks to Lasker's determination, we now consider blood pressure to be a significant measure of health. A recipient of the Presidential Medal of Freedom and Congressional Gold Medal for her work to support medical research, Lasker described herself as a normal woman who simply became a "self-employed health lobbyist."

Another hero in the battle against hunger and for better health was Dr. James Grant, who was the head of UNICEF from 1982 until 1995. A tireless proponent of saving children, Grant was responsible for a strategy that came to be known as GOBI: G for growth monitoring to detect undernutrition in small children; O for oral rehydration therapy to treat childhood diarrhea; B to encourage breastfeeding (which had declined precipitously due to working mothers and the marketing of infant formula); and I for immunization against the six basic childhood diseases: tuberculosis, polio, diphtheria, tetanus, whooping cough, and measles. (Three Fs—food supplements, family planning, and female education—were added later.)

Clearly there is a link between hunger, poverty, and health care. One of the strongest determinants of whether AIDS patients in South Africa (and elsewhere) will be able to lead independent lives is whether they will be able to eat decently. Several inspiring AIDS ministries in Cape Town and in Lubumbashi, the Democratic Republic of Congo, see the provision of food as being as significant as the availability of drugs.

In today's economy, as government budget cuts put new pressure on funding programs that benefit those in poverty, faith communities and nonprofit organizations have stepped forward with practical solutions to combat hunger and promote healthy lifestyles. A number of organizations have become adept at feeding the hungry by salvaging food that otherwise would be thrown away. Second Harvest is one such group that frequently utilizes the work of church and civic groups to save dented cans or otherwise perfectly good food for distribution to soup kitchens and food pantries. Through their diligent efforts and the generosity of individuals, they are providing a means to a healthy meal for those who would otherwise go without.

Questions for digestion

1. In what ways can you see that your health is a matter of social interaction rather than only an individual reaction? How does our culture encourage good health? Ill health? What do you think is meant by "holistic health"?
2. How are overconsumption and underconsumption both problems of justice? What does "honoring your body" imply about your health?

3

Appropriations and the Earth Community

Nothing underscores the extent to which all peoples, all species, and all other beings are interrelated better than the quality of our air and water—whether it is clean or hot or oily or oxygen-starved. Global warming has added its exclamation mark to this reality. No amount of money will enable anyone to opt out of that.

If you remember the packaged spinach scare of October 2006, you'll recall that the issue was traced back to a lethal strain of E. coli known as 0157:H7. This strain of bacteria was unknown before 1982; it is believed to have evolved in the guts of feedlot cattle standing around in their manure all day, eating a diet of grain that happens to turn a cow's rumen into an ideal habitat for the dangerous bacteria. Before 1982, that particular bug, now found in manure, couldn't survive in open pasture where cows lived. But the way in which livestock are raised in feedlots these days generates a lot of E. coli and other microbes that we kill off with pharmaceuticals. (Are you surprised?) In pastures, that manure could be promoting fertility.

"Wendell Berry once wrote that when we took animals off farms and put them onto feedlots, we had, in effect, taken an old solution—the one where crops feed animals and animals' waste feeds crops—and mostly divided it into two new problems: a fertility problem on the farm, and a pollution problem on the feedlot."[1] In effect, industrial agriculture and the way we eat now have created a new type of environmental hazard: food poisoning. And lots of spinach gets washed in the same "kitchens" and then packaged and shipped all over the place. It may be convenient just to cut open one of those packages of mixed greens, but the centralized food system that produced the salad may have delivered a lot of environmental hazards along with it.

Description: State of the Earth

Our stake in the health of the earth has become starkly obvious: everything that exists coexists. The primary focus of this chapter is the food supply system and how it has cost all of us some degree of the health of our planet. Most of our food is now produced by industrial agriculture, which has proved to be immensely productive, but at the cost of destroying its very means of production. (For example, consider our E. coli incident.) It has destroyed farmland, farm communities, and farmers. It wastes soil, water, energy, and life. Industrial agriculture is highly centralized, genetically impoverished, and dependent on cheap fossil fuels, on long-distance hauling, and on consumers' ignorance. Its characteristic by-products are erosion, pollution, and financial despair. This is an agriculture with a short future.

Industrial farming practices and the health of the land

Many industrial farming practices, while increasing production in the short run, run the risk of long-term damage to the earth. Current reports on global warming reflect the impact of this system of production. The increase in erosion and topsoil run-off has had dramatic effects in areas of our country. (Witness, for example, the wetlands below New Orleans and the greater impact that Hurricane Katrina had as a result of the reduction of their former retarding capacity, or consider the extent of the "dead zone" at the mouth of the Mississippi.) Crops are now genetically modified to grow twice their natural size, and we farm on land that is too dry for crops to grow, so it is irrigated with water diverted from rivers and lakes far away. Iron is mined and oil is drilled to manufacture and fuel the giant farm machinery that plows and fertilizes and harvests the monocrops that stretch far as the eye can see.

Fertilizer-dependent monocultures, planting the same few crops on the same ground year after year, deplete the soil's fertility and health in ways that are simply not sustainable. They also reduce natural defenses against disease and insect damage. Insecticides and pesticides must be ever intensified and reformulated to keep ahead of the pests. In 1992, Cornell University professor David Pimenthel calculated that U.S. farmers spend some $4 billion annually on pesticides to protect about $16 billion of crops. Doing so creates extra costs passed on to society at large—medical care for farmworkers' pesticide-induced cancers, fishery losses, the shortfall in honey production caused by dead bees, and more. The final price tag? Another $8 billion.[2]

Furthermore, our food system uses vast amounts of petroleum to transport food. Among the craziest dynamics is that at the same time California is exporting $18 million of asparagus, it is also importing $38 million worth of asparagus; New York ships $1.1 million worth of California almonds *to* Italy while importing exactly the same amount of almonds *from* Italy! Fruits, vegetables, and flowers all travel long distances, and each mile traveled increases the amount of greenhouse gas emissions into our atmosphere. Some have described beef as a petroleum by-product. Livestock producers use fossil fuels to plant seed in order to feed livestock, to produce and apply fertilizers and pesticides, and to harvest and process the feed. Electricity, gas, and diesel fuel are needed to maintain the animals and transport them to feedlots and then to meatpacking plants. More is used to process and package the meat and to refrigerate the trucks that haul it to distribution centers and then to our friendly grocery store.

Between 16 and 20 percent of all energy consumed in the United States is used by the food system, where the average food item travels upwards of 1,500 miles. This produces an enormous amount of CO_2, far more than would be the case with locally grown foods. Most disconcerting to me is the sheer quantity of energy calories it takes to produce, process, package, and distribute food to our homes. A can of corn requires 6 calories of such energy for every calorie of food energy it produces.[3] The food industry requires 10 calories of fossil fuel energy for each calorie of food energy it produces.

One final example comes from Dickson, Tennessee, where I used to lead worship when I was in grad school. Toxic chemicals polluted the pristine water that was once drawn from the Holt family well, and the family is persuaded that the groundwater is responsible for the death of several of its members. Assured by government officials that the water was safe in 1991, records reveal that dangerous levels of trichloroethylene existed in the water as early as 1988. Said Dr. Robert Bullard, director of the

Environmental Justice Resource Center at Clark Atlanta University: "The city and county fathers singled out this small, rural and mostly black Eno Road community to locate their garbage dumps, landfills, transfer stations, toxic waste sites, you name it. These waste sites are all located on Eno Road."[4] Such environmental racism often occurs in connection with growing crops. The sheer quantity of the wastes our agriculture produces and their impact on the environment are staggering. This waste and pollution can be partially trucked away from our residences, but only at the cost of someone else's residence. Finally, no one can completely outsource this waste. Wastes have to be distributed somehow and somewhere.

Animal health

The animals we eat and enjoy in other ways are significant members of our earth community; their health and ours are tied together. Yet we often practice cruelty to domestic animals in a way that escapes conscious attention. Even the way we feed animals is not their natural diet. Instead, we use synthetic fertilizers and oil-powered tractors to grow corn or soybeans that we then feed to cows, hogs, or chickens as an efficient substitute for grass, worms, and seeds. When we feed grains and soybeans to animals, we lose most of the grain's nutritional value. The animals use it to keep their bodies warm and to develop bones and other body parts that we cannot eat. Pig farms use six pounds of grain for every pound of boneless meat we get from them. For cattle in feedlots, the ratio is 13:1. Even for chickens, the least inefficient factory-farmed meat, the ratio is 3:1. To be clear, I am questioning two things here: one is the inefficiency and waste involved in feeding livestock the corn, soybeans, oats, and wheat that are humanly edible and not efficient for livestock and that require much fossil fuel to produce. Cattle, chickens, and hogs are not well served by that diet. Second, people in the United States do eat too much meat and not enough fruit, vegetables, and grains as it is.

Livestock has become a commodity for us. Industrialized agriculture has turned the production of our "edibles" away from cooperating with nature and into a high-cost system of always trying to overwhelm nature.

All these factors of livestock production are part of a system of food distribution and waste removal that is costly to the environment. When it comes to the question of how things should be distributed, religion professor and ethicist Kent Van Til reminds us that there is no perfect abstract distribution; all distributions are located at a particular time and place. According to Van Til, "The notion of distribution versus redistribution is a fiction. There is no pristine state of distribution from which all other arrangements are unjust redistributions. Goods are always flowing. Where would our original state of distribution begin? Would it begin before our European ancestors took the land from the North American Indians? Would it begin before the egregious accounting scandals at Enron that left thousands without pensions? . . . Would it begin before we were in the United States and before others were born in Central America?"[5]

It is also clear that the United States and China are the two countries responsible for the majority of CO_2 emissions in the world. Only Luxembourg has more CO_2 emissions per capita than the United States. Australia, Canada, and Finland are not far behind us.[6] Suffice it to say that we are complicit in generating the illness of the earth, and in two ways: by our own level of consumption (and the pollution it generates) and also by the products that we purchase that are outsourced to places such as Mexico, China, the Philippines, and India. In short, we are complicit by reason of enjoying what spoils our own and other people's air and water. No other example so vividly persuades me that our well-being and others' (of all species) are joined at the hip. Our futures are so much the same that money can buy only brief respite.

The implications of appropriation for happiness

I certainly do not like to think of myself as someone who contributes to the poor quality of air that afflicts a generation vulnerable to asthma, or to foods whose production entails the suffering of animals and my fellow species members. In fact, I try to avoid such a self-image. And yet my lifestyle clearly benefits from a disproportionate draw on the earth community. I am the problem—or at least a part of it; certainly corporately, top-feeding consumers like me are the problem.

I'm sure we don't intentionally set out to harm the health of our planet. That would be self-destructive. But wishful thinking does not take away our complicity in the problem. Like me, you probably try to compensate by recycling, frequenting farmers' markets, and avoiding the most heinously produced meats. Most people (who are able to) are willing to spend a little more for items that we think leave a softer footprint on our natural world. Good for us! But this is hardly a matter for bourgeois half steps. The point of all those studies that ask how much we would spend to be more ecologically responsible is one that is often overlooked: we know we are connected; how we spend does impact our future.

Our unwilling complicity in further befouling our home is killing us. Margaret Swedish, in her new book, *Living beyond the "End of the World": A Spirituality of Hope*, argues that in fact our way of life is killing us.[7] Literally, it is killing the planet. Changing our spirituality and our worldview is crucial to avoiding further decline. We are simply courting disaster by not changing. We wait for the levees to break and the waters to rise before we flee to higher ground.

We might consider two responses to the environmental degeneration we are seeing all around us. The first is a personal and individual change in consumer habits. A change in consumer habits might result in corporations resisting the change, co-opting the system, and simply finding other ways to continue production. But it might also result in a corporate response that would change the way we govern ourselves and the way we eat.

Part of the issue is that our supercapitalism is separating us into individual consumers. An aspect of the culture of consumption is that our desires are trained toward material aspirations. It is clear that material aspirations are individually based, and they almost always cast a blind eye to the health of the earth community, at least relatively speaking. Complicity accompanies material aspirations. (If our socialization has been successful, we see the health of the environment merely as another item to deal with, a detriment that we will attend to only fleetingly.)

Psychologist Timothy Kasser has done extensive research and compiled a book of studies on the impact of material aspirations. Material and income aspirations are a significant aspect of personal well-being. Studies done in the United States and Switzerland have found that our happiness depends primarily on our income relative to our income aspirations—and income aspirations in turn depend heavily on the average income of the people where we live.[8] People adjust their expectations as their income rises. Once you have a Lexus, the next step is a Jaguar or a Bentley or a Rolls-Royce.

What is the impact of rising expectations and aspirations? Put another way, what is the impact of always wanting more? Many people feel as though they always need more than they have to be happy. Those are the true believers in the economy of consumption, and they are culturally subject to forces that have taught them always to want more. Our wishes become wants, and our wants become needs, and our necessities become desires. The cycle of discontent and rising expectations keeps the economy spinning.

Kasser's collection of research on aspirations can be found in a book titled *The High Price of Materialism*. What is new about Kasser's treatise is the report that "merely *aspiring* to have greater wealth or more material possessions is likely to be associated with increased personal *un*happiness."[9] Though I am sure that while many people have successfully resisted the enticement of advertising and discounting and easy credit and psychological allure, most of us are subject to such temptations at least part of the time.

Kasser points to the cultural impact of generating aspirations in consumers and the influence of the aspirations themselves. He reports that studies of this phenomenon have consistently found that "people who strongly value the pursuit of wealth and possessions report lower psychological well-being than those who are less concerned with such aims."[10] So those who consider financial success a central value have lower levels of self-actualization and vitality and higher levels of depression and anxiety. This even has an impact on physical health; those who consider it important to strive for possessions, popularity, and good looks experience more headaches, backaches, sore muscles, and sore throats. Research has found that materialistic people are more possessive of their things (less willing to share them or rent them), are less generous, and are also envious of others.[11]

Furthermore, Kasser theorizes that four sets of needs are basic to the motivation, functioning, and well-being of all humans. They are:

- safety, security, and sustenance;
- competence, efficacy, and self-esteem;
- connectedness or relationship; and
- autonomy and authenticity.

The major portion of his book is spent examining the impact of materialistic aspirations on these four basic psychological needs. What he reports from his own work and that of others is that an orientation to materialistic values works against or undermines attaining these four needs. Not only do these values negatively affect the holders, but they also harm the health and happiness of others. Less empathy and intimacy is present in relationships, materialistic values are more likely to be transmitted to the next generation, and the health of the planet suffers with the adoption of more consumptive values.

Author, educator, and environmentalist Bill McKibben echoes Kasser's report in asserting that living as we do is simply unsustainable for the earth and its peoples. "We must share our bounty with the rest of the world," writes McKibben, "finding somewhere a middle ground so they do not follow our path to consumer development."[12] Additionally, David Myers, a psychology professor at Hope College and expert in happiness studies, has examined the impact of affluence on youth. According to Myers, "Wealth, like income, has been flooding upward, not trickling down," and we as a nation are growing more unhappy and depressed. "Today's youth and young adults have grown up with much more affluence, slightly less overall happiness, much greater risk of depression, and a tripled teen suicide rate. Never has a culture experienced such physical comfort combined with such psychological misery. Never have we felt so free or had our prisons so overstuffed. Never have we been so sophisticated about pleasure or so likely to suffer broken relationships."[13]

Material aspirations and consumption are individualistic and lead to distrust and a failure to love others. It is difficult to avoid the conclusion that overconsumption itself produces a sense of complicity. The major part of this problem is that in facing the world of nature, we assume that we can opt out if we have sufficient resources. However, individualism is not an option—for long. We are part and parcel of the community; in fact, we are very significant players in the community.

It is important for us as Christians and as believers in any earth-friendly ethic to believe that a different world is possible. It is possible, but only if we at the deepest level change our assumptions from those of privileged individualists to those of an eco-spiritual community. We have to uncover—as many theologians, historians, ecologists, scientists, and humanists are doing—that we are at base fellow creatures whose well-being is dependent on that of others. We need to act corporately, politically, and economically as a body to treat all life as interconnected.

Theological perspective: The unity of creation

We are part of the earth community right down to our toenails. The late Dr. Loren Eiseley, professor of anthropology and history of science at the University of Pennsylvania, spoke about the "web of life." He was right—we are all interconnected. Similarly, Larry Rasmussen, social ethics professor at Union Theological Seminary, asserts that we were "born to belonging." We are biological-social beings who depend on others for all manner of things from the womb onward. For some years at the outset of our lives, we simply could not survive without others. According to Rasmussen, "We stand on the shoulders of ancestors, compatriots, and anonymous millions. Our own journey begins with their legacy. Not least, when dying day comes, and we return to the topsoil we are, we will join in yet another way the great community of life that birthed us. We are born into belonging, and we die in it."[14] Christians believe that God created us in this way and that God created us good. Every part of the earth community is interconnected in such a way that together we form a home for each other. This includes *all* species, not only the human one. The cosmos was made, we believe, so that all life could flourish.

Three words articulate this sense that all life is created to flourish together. One is *ubuntu* from the Zulu language. As I understand the word, it basically means the recognition that my welfare is dependent on yours and yours is dependent on mine. Thus, two people meet in the street: One might say, "How are you?" The reply may be, "I am well if you are well." *Ubuntu.* This awareness of how my welfare and yours are interconnected is not only a wonderful sentiment; it is also true. The more advanced ecological science becomes, the more it is clear that all natural beings are dependent on each other for their sustainability and flourishing. The success and pervasive affirmation of Al Gore's film, *An Inconvenient Truth*, made this evident in regard to global warming.

Another word is *jeong*, a Korean term that can be associated with "heart," "compassion," and "vulnerability." When used as a verb, *jeong* connotes "arising, emerging out of in-between-ness." Thus, there is a genesis of becoming that is intimately linked with connectedness and heart. It suggests an ongoing process of incarnation. What is interesting to me about the word is that it can be used to indicate an ability of the oppressor to empathize with the oppressed, to understand another person's plight.

According to theologian W. Anne Joh, "*Jeong* actively calls us to recognize the Self in the Other as a form of collaborative compassion."[15] But Joh also warns that this quality tends to be "uncomfortable" for Western individualistic sensibilities.

The capstone word is the Hebrew *shalom*, which we often translate as "peace." *Shalom* is a particular type of peace, the peace of all the parts working well together in the sort of harmony that God intended in creation. The biblical vision of *shalom* is that all of creation is one, every creature in community with every other, living in harmony and security toward the joy and well-being of every other creature. *Shalom* then can be translated "wholeness" or "completeness," and, while the word specifies a corporate and holistic unity, it also implies that we were created for personal "wholeness" within the entirety.

It may be well to repeat what I wrote earlier about the logic of this theological belief. It is a belief, but one that describes reality as it is rather than only as one wishes or believes it to be. In short, the world is arranged by *shalom*, is created in *shalom*, and we flourish when we are in *shalom*. This theological conviction is increasingly reinforced by ecological science. The interconnection of creation, the unity of being, is as much fact as belief, and its regeneration as much a necessity to survival as a goal.

Moral directions

Food systems are at the heart of *ubuntu*, *jeong*, and *shalom*. Our planet has a global food system as well as local food systems that diverge and overlap. In what moral directions does the theological perspective on the unity of creation point?

One overarching direction arises from the belief that God wills that everyone have a sufficiency, that everyone have enough to sustain and enjoy their lives. That seems clear from the Gospel accounts of Jesus' life and ministry, and it is a major thread throughout the Scriptures. God loves all that God has created and wills the good for them. The cosmos is interconnected and God wills that all flourish.

In short, a global ethic needs to articulate those directions and goals that make for the good for *all*, not only the majority and not only the affluent. This means that all beings count for one, but not more than one. The well-being of others has priority over the luxury of choice for the affluent. But the affluent do count for one.

This book has already looked at two notions of fair treatment or justice: distributive justice, which aims to ensure that goods and services are fairly divided, and just relations—that all people get treated in a way appropriate to their being human beings. A third norm, *sustainable justice,* expresses our relationship with nature. In some ways sustainability requires some attention to restorative justice for the earth in those places and systems where the harm done will continue without intervention. Restorative justice involves the effort to restore environmental and social conditions to a decent level of quality. It is to rectify, or "make right," what has become disordered. Energy, for example, is an area where conservation and development of renewable sources should be part of restorative justice. The practice of stripping off the tops of mountains for their coal is unsustainable and may be irreversible. In fact, almost all irreversible actions are by definition unsustainable.

Restorative justice is not a term that comes trippingly to the tongue; nevertheless, what it expresses is that many people and other natural systems are not blank slates. None of us start from zero in this world; we are born into countries and parents and economies that have specific life-chances. There are natural systems and peoples who have been systematically disadvantaged and who live in situations that, if left to themselves, will only get worse.

It is vital, as we know, that the earth be treated as an organism whose full life and well-being cannot be assumed any longer. We simply must understand that we live together on this ball. We are part of the system that will perish without sustainable actions. Important as our attention to the health of the planet is, included within that will need to be sustainable community development of societies and peoples. Indeed, the whole web is the audience that we must address; every restorative action must take the health of the whole into account.

I believe this norm means that our economy will have to be bent in the direction of more sustainable means of production. We will have to find ways to reuse and recycle, or not use some things at all. Sustainability will need to be the trump card. Otherwise, we will continue to suffer the tsunamis, hurricanes, tornadoes, and other natural catastrophes whose intensity appears to be furthered by our inattention to natural protections.

In a way this norm expresses our relationship to nature as the other three forms of justice—restorative, distributive, and contributive—support our relationship with other people. But in a larger sense, the whole apparatus of the earth community and its possibilities for justice depend on our finding a way and a will to live in a sustainable fashion.

Steps toward transformation

There is no scarcity of ideas about how to "green" the world these days. (As though it wasn't already!) However, evidence about the melting of the Arctic icecap and rising water levels in island nations has persuaded me that we have less time to do something about this than we thought. There is no crevice into which the state of the environment has not found its way; it has become clear to us that the earth community is pervasive. Droughts and famines accompany each other; our TVs bring us images of what happens to people and cattle during this crisis. Politically and economically, the state of Zimbabwe, which was an agriculturally verdant country in 1990 and is now experiencing significant malnutrition and starvation, gives evidence that the environment feels such upheaval—and that we are part of that environment.

A very hopeful signal is that many of the religions of the world are recovering a concern for the environment, a concern that has been deeply woven into their traditions but has been neglected. The concern for a sustainable earth community can be found in Buddhist and Baha'i teachings that stress the "middle way" between excess and deprivation and emphasize obligations to the preservation of nature. "Socially engaged" Buddhism in Asia and the United States is active in forest conservation, and Hindus are especially concerned to preserve rivers and waterways. Rabbi Goldie Milgram, executive director of Reclaiming Judaism as a Spiritual Practice, notes that three Jewish commandments could help supply the rationale and parameters for keeping eco-kosher. The injunction not to waste could be applied to food packaging, for example. At Colegio Santa Maria, a private Roman Catholic school in Sao Paulo, Brazil, the Sisters of the Holy Cross have integrated environmental concerns into their curriculum and lifestyles.

Kentucky author and conservationist Wendell Berry suggests that if Christians were to "take seriously those passages in the scripture that say that we live by God's spirit and his breath, that we live, move, and have our being in God, the implications for the present economy are just devastating. Those passages call for an entirely generous and careful economic life."[16] It is true that many religious organizations are taking this perspective with great seriousness, and others have sprung up that take as their founding mission the preservation of the quality of earth community. In response, hundreds of congregations across the country have conducted energy assessments to determine if they have maximized their use of renewable energy and cut as much use of nonrenewable energy as possible. These faithful congregations are working to conserve both finances and the state of the planet. They are among the many hopeful signs throughout our culture.

Questions for digestion

1. Our culture of consumption—the system we enjoy— involves a great deal of waste: pollution of the air and water; stuff that winds up in landfills; and vast quantities of food waste. Can you suggest both *why* this is so and *how* we could begin to remedy it?

2. People may continue to live in ways that make the earth community secondary to their own comfort out of *fear* of not having enough. If everyone were *guaranteed* sufficient goods to have an adequate standard of living, how would that enable us to see the connections in the web of creation, to live with *ubuntu* and *jeong* in light of *shalom*?

4

Cheap Food, Rural Communities, and Farming

Our cheap food policies have decimated many rural communities and have weakened those that still depend on farming. I remember Old Testament scholar Walter Brueggemann giving a paper in Riverside Church in New York on the way that the city was dependent on the countryside. Brueggemann called the relationship parasitic, and he claimed that nothing about that dynamic had changed from the days of the Hebrew Scriptures until today.

A November 2007 issue of *Time* included an article titled "Down on the Farm." The subhead read "U.S. agricultural policy is bad for the country's economy, environment, global image and rural towns. But don't expect it to change anytime soon."[1] This was in *Time* magazine—we are *not* talking about a radical journal here, folks. The text of the article—looking at the Farm Bill—could as easily have talked about "food policy" as "agricultural policy." (As a matter of fact, *New York Times* columnist Nick Kristof has suggested that the Secretary of Agriculture should be renamed the Secretary of Food!) The Farm Bill is really about controlling the price of our food, and that is the sensitive political issue.

Description: The cost to rural communities and farmers

Less than 3 percent of all farms produce more than a half million dollars worth of crops annually; they produce almost 60 percent of all commodities ultimately sold in grocery stores and restaurants. The most striking shift in farm size, according to the Economic Research Service, is toward very large family farms; 75 percent of U.S. production comes from 5.6 percent of farms, according to the 2007 Census of Agriculture.[2] These are large-scale operations that may be operated by a family with one or two hired hands, but they hardly fit the nostalgic ma-and-pa image. More typically and increasingly, these large farms are under contract to produce livestock or crops according to corporate specifications. While the absolute number of "farms" grew from 2002 to the present, 41.6 percent of them were classed as "limited-resource," "retirement," or "residential/lifestyle." The share of production on smaller family farms (less than $250,000 in annual sales) fell from 26 percent in 2003 to 21.2 percent in 2007.[3] These farms may still be classified as family-operated, but they do not depend on their farming operations to provide a major portion of family income. Thirty-five percent of all farms each produce less than $2,500 in sales annually.[4]

What all these statistics clearly state is that farm operations are getting bigger or they are getting much smaller; the independent family owner-operator farmer who is making a living from farming is a rarity these days. Middle-range operations are emptying out. Crop and livestock production is shifting to very large farms. Furthermore, when one looks at operating margins, the average profit margin for all farms with less than $250,000 in sales is negative. For farms with less than $10,000, there was a -98 percent margin; for farms with $10,000 to $99,999 there was a -24.8 percent margin; and for farms with sales between $100,000 and $249,999 there was a -1.8 percent margin.[5] Farms with larger sales averaged +10.6, +16.4, and +15.3 percent margins.

In short, fewer people per acre operate farms these days. What that translates into is the loss of farmers and the businesses that accompany farming (the sale of farm equipment, seeds, fertilizer, feed, and pesticides) in most rural communities. That also translates into the loss of families and other businesses and services, loss of voluntary organizations, loss of congregations, and loss of the power to attract the children of rural communities to return to their home communities.

It is true that many rural communities are rebounding these days and finding niche markets in recreation, tourism, specialty crops, ethanol, and off-site electronic offices. That is all to the good. But what those averages overlook is the fact that more poverty exists in rural communities than in urban ones, the infant mortality rate is higher, and the number of people on some form of assistance is greater. The incidence of suicide also deserves mention. While suicide is the eleventh-ranking cause of death nationwide, it is the second leading cause of trauma-related deaths in states with primarily rural populations, especially states in the rural mountain West and Alaska. The communities with these negative quality-of-life indicators are likely to be formerly agricultural ones found in the broad swath of the middle of the United States. There, hunger and poverty persist.

What has happened to those formerly idyllic small towns in the bucolic countryside is a direct result of our agribusiness-favoring cheap food policy. It is not only the farmers in

Mexico who are going out of business; it is farmers in the United States who have farmed until their equity has run out or their spouses (usually wives) have said, "Enough already. We are selling out and moving to Arizona or Florida." We who live in cities, who buy our food at Wal-Mart, Kroger, Hy-Vee, and Albertsons, are benefiting from the very forces that have produced poverty in many rural communities. I know that is stark, but it is true.

In a truly remarkable display of irony, our cheap food policy has produced skyrocketing costs to the national budget as well, a budget that is way out of balance anyway. Vincent A. Gallagher, in a book titled *The True Cost of Low Prices*, quotes a *Business Week* editorial indicating that "the United States, Europe, and Japan spend $300 billion a year to subsidize farmers."[6] Besides undercutting local markets in Pakistan, Indonesia, and other parts of the developing world, this subsidy costs U.S. taxpayers enormously. That money is supporting the bottom lines of Cargill, Smithfield, Bunge, and ADM.

The same *Time* article mentioned at the beginning of this chapter contained a graph showing that only 39 percent of farms receive a subsidy at all. Of that 39 percent, the top 10 percent receive an "average annual payment per recipient" of $34,190. The average for the bottom 80 percent was $704! Averages are of course deceptive, but I think that statistic means that a husband and wife in the top 10 percent receive a household subsidy of $68, 380 on average, and those in the bottom 80 percent get $1,408. A lot is wrong in Kansas.

There are other associated costs: I have pointed to the expenses that we experience and pay as a result of our poor health, including the costs that we incur from the medical and life insurance industry. Additionally, we experience the ill will that comes from developing countries that find that their local food economy is being undercut by U.S. trade policies. No doubt there are other costs, but let us leave this chronicle at that.

In regard to complicity, it is important for us to note that citizens are implicated in the system this chapter has described even if and when we feel we have no choice. Americans are simply born into a situation in which they participate. There is no transcendent realm from which we gain the distance to stand apart from the social situation. We enjoy cheap food. Others produce that food cheaply. This is, as has become obvious, a collective issue in which the nation as a whole experiences social agency.

The food production sector of our economy is sustained significantly through the work of agricultural workers. Some harvest the crop while others are employed in meat and poultry processing plants. Many are immigrant peoples or other "minority" peoples; some are immigrants from Mexico, Central America, or Southeast Asia. These workers do the work that many Americans would not do.

Clearly there are farmers and ranchers who do provide just compensation to farmworkers, but in many cases the working conditions, wages, living accommodations, and services for workers are substandard. Migrants may "come with the dust and leave with the wind" and often experience a number of interrelated problems: poverty, inadequate housing, poor sanitation, environmental hazards, inadequate health care, lack of educational opportunities, and nonexistent child labor laws.

Working conditions in meat and poultry processing plants need to be included in farmworker discussions. Jobs in poultry processing plants are exceedingly dangerous. The author of *Fast Food Nation*, Eric Schlosser, has detailed what goes on in many slaughterhouses and writes, "Once you learn how our modern industrial food system has transformed what most Americans eat, you become highly motivated to eat something else. . . . Tyson ads don't show chickens crammed together at the company's factory farms, and Oscar Mayer ads don't reveal what really goes into those wieners."[7]

New York Times columnist Bob Herbert's report "Where the Hogs Come First" gives you a taste of this. He asks us to think about pork, bacon, breakfast sausage, juicy chops, and ribs—exactly what is packed at Smithfield Packing Company in Tar Heel, North Carolina. "You can learn a lot at Smithfield," he writes. "It's a case study in both the butchering of hogs (some 32,000 are slaughtered there every day) and the systematic exploitation of vulnerable workers. More than 5,500 men and women work at Smithfield, most of them Latino or black, and nearly all of them undereducated and poor."[8] The issue at Smithfield is not the money so much as the work, which "is often brutal beyond imagining. . . . Serious injuries abound, and the company has used illegal and, at times, violent tactics over the course of a dozen years to keep the workers from a union that would give them a modicum of protection and dignity." One of the workers reports, "You have to work fast because that machine is shooting those hogs out at you constantly. You can end up with all this blood dripping down on you, all these feces and stuff just hanging off of you. It's a terrible environment." Those conditions are an integral part of the cheap food we enjoy. Suddenly that bacon doesn't sound so appealing.

There is much more that could be said in describing the cost of our cheap food policy to rural communities, small farmers, and farmworkers. Perhaps it will be enough to note the inequality that prevails in our carefully disguised but greatly stratified class society in rural America. Bread for the World reports that the "average income of 'very large farms' specializing in [welfare subsidy] program crops is $329,859, more than 50 times the average incomes of households receiving food stamps ($7,776)." Furthermore, "A household of three must have an annual income of less than $21,588 to be eligible for food stamps. Commodity payment recipients may have an adjusted gross income of up to $2.5 million—116 times greater than a food stamp applicant—to remain eligible for farm payments."[9]

The implications of appropriation for happiness

Excuse me, but do you find the above information somewhat incredible as well? Perhaps we are used to such inequality and injustice. However, let us pursue the consequences for our well-being of the appropriation that such inequalities represent. What does it mean that we participate in a society that systematically and legislatively disadvantages some communities for a higher standard of living for others?

Two British researchers have addressed this question by researching the impact of inequality. Epidemiologists Richard Wilkinson and Kate Pickett report what we have already learned: the wider the society's gaps between the affluent and everyone else, the more sickly the entire society. As they report in the November 2007 issue of *Social Science and Medicine*, "As inequality increases so does poor health."[10]

This rather conventional finding simply means that the richer you are, the better health you enjoy. However, Wilkinson and Pickett's findings go beyond health. Other social problems are associated with income inequality. In their paper, the two researchers pore over data from twenty-four major developed nations on social problems that range from drug abuse to educational performance. The evidence, they conclude, helps establish the simple but important point that numerous social problems associated with relative deprivation—from ill health to poor educational performance—are more common in more unequal societies. These differences were not trivial; they found a "ten-fold difference in homicide rates between more and less equal countries and U.S. states, six-fold differences in teenage birth rates, six-fold differences in the prevalence of obesity, four-fold differences in how much people feel they can trust each other."[11]

To profit from the low prices that farmers receive for their products and to be the (however indirect) cause of rural communities' gradual decline cannot produce happiness. There is a direct connection between the economic sustainability of farm families, especially those who operate midsized farms, their neighbors in rural communities, and the earth community of soil and water and forestlands. It is clear that the well-being of rural communities and the well-being of the ecosphere are linked. Many rural people are obese, ironically enough, because they live in "food deserts" like the one in Orange County, South Carolina, where convenience store food is far more readily accessible than good fruit and vegetables. I would be remiss to portray this situation as hopeless; it is not. However, it is also clear that the way that the resources of rural communities have been appropriated domestically is exactly the same process that has brought us cheap products from China, India, Taiwan, and the Philippines. We simply cannot feel happy about benefiting from the decimation of rural communities and farmers, whether in Mexico or in Missouri. However, there are numerous ways to rectify this situation.

Happiness or well-being apparently cannot be successfully pursued directly, but that has not kept us from pursuing it via money, success, prestige, and possessions. This appears, according to David Bornstein, author of *How to Change the World*, to be exactly the wrong formula. Instead, our well-being seems to result from serving others. "Perhaps," writes Bornstein, "we can learn from 'social entrepreneurs' who depart from the conventional pathways of success in order to devote themselves to solving social problems. What happens when a person pursues a path of action that aligns with his or her interests, talents, and values and also contributes to the well-being of others?"

Bornstein goes on to give examples of social entrepreneurs who have done exactly that. Some of the pleasures such entrepreneurs mention in following this course include "obtaining justice for a disadvantaged person," "creating something of beauty where nothing before existed," "feeling part in some way of human beings' overcoming challenges and thriving," "spending time with family, "collaborating with colleagues to solve problems, and "having experiences that affirm a sense of oneness with the world." Perhaps the strongest theme was "actualizing and witnessing the growth of others' potential—using your life to enable the life in others to flourish."[12] In this way, people found themselves to be happy.

Theological perspective: A breakdown in *shalom*

It is not too much to invoke Paul's words to the Corinthians to describe the place of farming and rural communities in our society. "Indeed, the body does not consist of one member but of many. . . . God arranged the members in the body, each one of them, as he chose. . . . The members of the body that seem to be weaker are indispensable. . . . If one member suffers, all suffer together with it" (1 Cor. 12:14, 18, 22, 26). In short, the whole body of the society needs rural communities and farmers if it is to thrive. Without the basic necessity of food, where would the society be? Without farmers, where would we find sustenance?

Without farmers, what would be the quality of our food, our ponds, our wildlife, our air, our appreciation of the land, and our community?

In a real sense, rural communities, farmers, and farmworkers are parts of the body—perhaps seen as weaker or less honorable or inferior by some—but nevertheless indispensable. In fact, these people are representatives of the whole society as they bring to the whole the careful production of food, the care of local environments, and many gifts of appreciation that the wider society needs.

Rather than these members of the body being treated with the care they deserve, however, they have been treated as colonies. Their futures are not their own; prices and regulations are set far from the site of production. The competitive free-enterprise system has become ruthless in its quest for cheap goods. They are simply collateral damage. That is the perception; the reality is that we all suffer together when the rural part of the body is decimated.

In contrast to the abundance that God gives to us all—an abundance that translates at the least into a sufficiency of goods—these parts of the country have been shortchanged. Their economic affairs have been arranged to serve others rather than themselves. They have been treated with a strict laissez-faire attitude—"whatever we can get away with, and the less the better." Rather than being shown the grace and love of God, these people have not even been treated with respect, the minimum requirement of justice.

The breakdown of *shalom* is evident here. However, it is important to recall the ideal society wherein people are treated with fairness and everyone is accorded the respect and dignity that are due them simply as children of God. We imagine a harmonious whole in which all creatures are treated with the goodness that builds up all the other parts of the system. That is what Christians ask for when they pray, "Your kingdom come. Your will be done, on earth as it is in heaven" (Matt. 6:10). In Daoism, it is in the nature of things that they seek a harmony. This harmony is not static. In it there is a differentiation and at the same time determination, because it constantly seeks Dao. That is the *summum bonum*. One facet of the Lord's Supper is an egalitarian sharing of Christ's body in the humility that is appropriate to our having been graced and called to participate together. Insofar as the Eucharist is the model for our eating all meals, we attempt during this practice to commune toward the way food will be distributed in the kingdom of heaven, without money and without price. In true egalitarianism all are well fed and flourish. Insofar as our ideal falls short of that, we are to work for an enjoyable and equitable life here on earth as in heaven.

Moral directions: Contributive and distributive justice

We can begin to work toward the ideal by enunciating moral directions that bring us closer to that. One of those, perhaps surprisingly, is that of contributive justice.

Contributive justice expresses our privilege of working in ways that make a contribution to society and also to our enjoyment. Our vocations, the way we spend our time, and how we mediate the grace of God that has been given to us are ways that we give back or, better yet, give on to others. We are able to give our time, our energy, and our ability to others in ways that we find fulfilling. Too long has work been seen as drudgery. Let's face it: there is drudgery, but for most of us—certainly most of the affluent—our work is challenging and fulfilling.

This norm also expresses the fact that everyone should have an opportunity to make a contribution to the society. Welfare and dependency are not satisfying. Everyone should be able to participate in building up the well-being of the society. In so doing we are finding our vocations and receiving a sense of belonging to the community even as we give.

Rural communities and farmers should not have to receive welfare or subsidies that render many of their operations subject to political currents. Just as they did for other workers, the governing bodies are to enable these workers to make a decent living, not detract from their ability or make their working conditions intolerable.

For those who have control over the distribution of benefits and liabilities, the norm to guide their policy and action is that of *distributive justice*. This is nothing more or less than simple fairness. Hard work and careful production are to be rewarded, at least with a decent standard of living. Taking advantage of farmworkers is anything but just; it violates their dignity as human beings.

An overarching ideal that is both imaginable and also reflects a basic level of justice is that of the "just price." What should go into a just price? Dr. Albino Barrera, a theologian at Providence College, has traced the history of the just price. He finds in the Old Testament a scriptural basis for economic rights within an economic security mandated by God. Barrera argues, "It is clear that the just price is about ensuring that people are provided with an income that secures access to their basic necessities."[13] The community was understood to be implicated in meeting this goal, as were individual men and women to the extent possible. One basis for the health of rural persons and communities is distributing income in such a way as to reflect just prices and wages.

Steps toward transformation

There are numerous positive signs that more and more people are beginning to understand that the health of agriculture and the health of the environment are interdependent, even in the United States, a country where less than 1.5 percent of the population are farmers. The recent debate about the Farm Bill was far more vigorous than previous tussles about the shape of that behemoth bill have been in the past. In large part, that is because we as a people are beginning to realize that food policy and agricultural policy are absolutely inseparable. There is a broader and broader audience whose voting habits will be determined by the stance politicians take on the earth community. Rural communities, farmers, and farmworkers play vital roles in maintaining, improving, or continuing the degeneration of the stratosphere we depend upon.

Former president George W. Bush proposed a number of significant and laudable reforms in the last Farm Bill. For one thing, he proposed capping the amount of subsidy that any single farming unit can receive at $200,000—far less than the current million-dollar cap. For another, and directly related to our hungry world, Bush proposed that $300 million could be shifted from farm subsidies to enable global governments and relief groups to buy food locally rather than from U.S. sources and shipped in U.S. ships. This would enable starving people in the arid reaches of northwestern Kenya, for example, to gain access to food far more quickly than their desperate circumstances allowed. While $300 million may not be sufficient overall, for those who are starving, it means receiving food aid in time.

There is much encouraging progress being made internationally as numerous nongovernmental organizations (NGOs) get involved. Jeffrey Sachs and the U.N.-backed Millennium Village initiative have helped more than a dozen countries in sub-Saharan Africa receive aid from Millennium Promise. Business and civic leaders are contributing to this poverty-ending alliance, which promotes improved agriculture and holistic community development. In the Tanzanian village of Mbola, the first step has been to help farmers harvest more food by providing fertilizers and high-yield seeds.[14]

In the United States, consumers increasingly are taking decisions about what they will eat out of the hands of the giant retailers that control a majority share of certain commodities. More and more people in cities are growing some of their own food and are regaining access to food. For example, some groceries have joined Affiliated Foods, a cooperative arrangement where consumers themselves help shape policy. Do consumers want to be able to make decisions about what they will eat? Increasingly, it appears they do.

A new vision of what the food and farming system can be is developing. This vision celebrates uniqueness and diversity in the food system and promotes eating seasonally and eating locally. The place of taste is becoming more and more important. The principle that unites this vision is that of putting people first—on the farm, in the plant, and in the community. At the heart of this vision is the concept that food establishes a relationship and that people want relationships with their food—its growers, its chefs, its grocers, its nutrition, its soil and water, and the eaters who select it. This is the Food Circle image that Dr. Mary Hendrickson is promoting in Missouri and others are promoting in other states.

A community food system requires three things: (1) knowledge—how to cook, grow, process, market, and distribute food that is connected to a particular place and time;

(2) infrastructure—learning to rebuild our society and create transportation networks that are local and responsive to local conditions; and (3) adequate storage and retail space, as well as regulations, policies, and education that will respect the community. There may be a bit of "back-to-the-future" about this. This is the way that farming operated on a local scale, and those structures could be reformed and renewed.

How can we get food from the farm gate to the eater's plate? Many distribution centers and market outlets are emerging: upscale restaurants, farmers' markets (4,300 nationwide at latest count), congregation-sponsored farms, grocery stores featuring local products, and Web-based networks such as www .localharvest.org. Steps individuals can take include sharing food with others at meals and talking about food, bringing local foods to your church potluck, sharing raspberries with others (as my parishioner Virginia Green used to do), and sourcing one ingredient per meal from local places.

There are as many ways to support farmers and farmworkers and rural communities as there are imaginations. Suggest taking up the topic in a local book club or adult education class or church youth group. Do not underestimate the power of faith, and be willing to dialogue with others who may share more of your values than you think.

David Bornstein, in his inspiring book, *How to Change the World*, tells the story of Fabio Rosa in Brazil.[15] In Brazil's southernmost province, Rio Grande do Sul, there was a depressed area named Palmares where the primary wealth was the irrigated rice crop. Ninety percent of the land was lowland, good only for rice production. Rice needs a lot of water, but those who controlled the irrigation water were wealthy landowners who charged high prices for it.

Rosa found that rice had been irrigated in Louisiana in the 1940s with artesian wells. The only problem was that there was no rural electrification for pumping water in rural Brazil. Working with a friendly government official, Rosa found a way of developing inexpensive electrification through monophase electricity. The electricity was used to pump water from artesian wells, bringing it closer to the farming surface and enabling saturation flooding for the rice (a great environmental benefit). Soon the few hundred rice farmers who were able to use this system had multiplied their production many-fold. Fabio Rosa and his comrades had to work with and against the government; against the dominant electric company; and in conflict and cooperation with many other natural and political impediments. This was a long and arduous process.

However, following the electrification of much of rural Rio Grande do Sul, Rosa developed a solar electric system that he managed to implement across Brazil. With the development of cheap electricity, he also brought in rotational grazing. Such a system depends on being able to rotate cattle from one electrically fenced area to another before they destroyed the grass in the first one. The environmental and economic benefits are manifest.

Clearly Fabio Rosa is a social entrepreneur of persistence and imagination, and farmers throughout Brazil have benefited from his work. However, even Fabio Rosa cannot do only one thing. Like the Okies of John Steinbeck's *Grapes of Wrath*, millions of Brazilians had been migrating to shantytowns built on the edge of cities where unemployment and crime rates were creating massive social upheaval. Rosa attacked the root cause of this migration—the fact that farmers could not make a living in the countryside—and managed to ease the pressure to migrate. If this social entrepreneur and his partners could so dramatically change the prospects for farmers, farmworkers, and rural communities in Brazil, why not in the United States? Why not in other countries? While I do not want to be either naïve or unrealistically optimistic, there are already movements afoot that can result in a better future for farmers and farmworkers who often cannot afford to eat what they produce. Hunger in rural America is a problem, but the situation can be improved for rural communities and the people who live there. Our food system and its interlocking sectors—health, environment, and economics—can be changed. We the American consumers can take back our eating. As a matter of fact, this is already happening for many. Moreover, this possibility needs to be accessible for people without a lot of money who now have few choices. We can change federal policy and local action in such a way that they too will be able to enjoy the lives that God gave them in healthy, creative ways. The food supply system belongs to everyone.

Questions for digestion

1. The author speaks of what is happening to rural communities, farmers, and farmworkers as "collateral damage." Why do you think groups who produce as essential a product as food are treated so poorly?

2. How did you feel reading the story of what Fabio Rosa accomplished in Brazil? How do you feel when you buy locally—at a farmers' market or roadside stand? Are those feelings connected?

5

Losing and Refinding Our Spiritual Selves

The consequences of the cheap food policies we have been considering so far have been fairly concrete: poor nutrition, drain on rural communities, global inequities, and environmental pollution. But all these very definite and measurable consequences of our cheap food policy are part of a much wider phenomenon that affects our spiritual formation. In short, we live in a culture where it seems preferable to allow some people to be malnourished so long as we are doing well. It is evident from this that we are not as spiritually or corporately sensitive as we could be and were created to be. Christianity is engaged in battle with this false god of consumption that infiltrates our society. Likewise, Islam, Judaism, Buddhism, and Daoism fight against this spiritual emptiness. It may be that the world food crisis is interconnected with a spiritual one, and in this chapter we will examine ways to reverse course and affect positive change for ourselves and for our world.

Description: Spirituality lost

I grew up in Zachary, Louisiana, where there were lots and lots of pious words and biblical language. When I was nine, my dad and mom were called to be missionaries in the Belgian Congo, he as a dental missionary and she as a teacher. The contrast of those pious, sweet, quite segregated, fundamentalist words with the starkness of starvation, abscess, and illness among the Congolese impacted me greatly. I also reacted against spirituality as a whole, which I associated with inauthentic hypocrisy. Only recently have I been happy to have the language of spirituality de-pietized and reconstructed for me.

Spirituality, as I now think of it, is really about a hunger for relationships. Being an ethicist, I retained a concern for just relationships all those years, but now I am seeing that the strongest hunger, maybe even my strongest hunger, is for a relationship with God. I am still working out what that means, and I expect to be for the rest of my life.

The question really is "Who is in charge?" Am I in charge of creating my life and shaping it to my whims? I act like that. I try very hard to insure my life against all sorts of negative happenstances, and it seems, at least, as though I can. However, there are many instances where I know that only a hairbreadth has separated my family and me from terrible things. And, ultimately, I can see that I am going to die, just like my father, mother, parents-in-law, and our third embryo did.

I trust that you will excuse all this autobiography. It is my way of making the point that our capabilities, affluence (from the median U.S. income up), and lifestyle have eaten into our capacity for accepting or consenting to or acquiescing in a spirituality that is beyond our control. And a spirituality that is not beyond our control is not worth having. In short, I am talking about the quasi-spirituality that is the enemy of the authentic, that is, the spirituality of consumption and perhaps the most serious source of our complicity. It is the engine that keeps us from addressing the awful consequences our complicity permits, that finally gives power over us and erodes our well-being.

Finally, the desire to control reality is self-defeating. The more we attempt to control—and this is the promised capacity of affluence—the more we find such control elusive if not nonexistent. The desire to control is itself a disease that prevents us from discovering the security and joy we long for. The promise that consumption offers is at least partial control.

Speaking of consumption, I trust it is clear that I find myself exactly there as well. I am not trying to make you (or me) feel bad, but if you are like me, you really enjoy the convenience, comfort, and ease of your lifestyle. And that is the serious demon. We have been bought off; we have settled for ease and comfort when well-being is available.

There's a scene from the movie *What about Bob?* in which Bill Murray is a guest at a family dinner. He is seriously enjoying his meal. Loudly. Slurpingly. It's driving the dad (Richard Dreyfus) crazy. The wife loves it, the kids love it, but Dreyfus has finally had it. "Would you stop it!" he yells.

What I take away from that is that Dreyfus can't stand how much Murray is enjoying his meal. He is jealous of Murray's enjoyment. That's what I think happens to us, too. Our comfort jeopardizes our capacity to enjoy deeply and wholeheartedly and fully. And finally our inability will erode our well-being— excuse me, *is* eroding our well-being.

The implications of appropriation for happiness

At this point we turn to the consideration of how this issue (the state of our spiritual well-being) has impacted our happiness. Using social scientific data, we have been making the case that our complicity actually impairs or fatally invades our sense of well-being.

As understood by the social scientific researcher, happiness seems virtually always an individual term. However, the case we have been building is that it is not possible to experience well-being except relationally. Ironically, social scientists themselves have been instrumental in making the case that there are no unrelated or unconnected individuals, that life is at base relational. For example, the research of economists Bruno Frey and Alois Stutzer found that people who participate in institutions that encourage and support political participation are those who are happiest. That may be reported as an individual property rather than a relational one. However, it is important to consider whether the institution itself does not represent a set of relationships that encourages happiness.

There are blind spots in happiness studies. For example, there is little or no consideration of sin and evil, sacrifice and accountability. So Berkeley professor Judith Butler can speak of our participation in culture as always involving complicity and appropriation.[1] We are tied together with others, and only in that way can well-being emerge. This almost inevitably will involve sacrifice and accountability. Accountability is requisite to relationships. The neglect of these dimensions is, perhaps, understandable if happiness is taken to mean only a feeling or a momentary pleasure, but we are after bigger game here. There are aspects of life and meaning that are not subject to social scientific discovery.

To the extent that they are capable of doing so, happiness studies do seem to support the thesis we are advancing. But they cannot establish a correlation between complicity and lack of well-being because their data collection is individual, not systemic. Because they define happiness in a particular way, these studies skew the data, making it difficult to uncover the relational dynamic and how that feeds into well-being.

The question of what makes for happiness is one in which we are all interested, and I will offer you what evidence and findings there are.

Lord Richard Layard, one of Britain's most prominent economists and a world expert on unemployment and inequality, tackles this very question as a social policy and not simply an individual question. While he holds that we all desire happiness and agree the best society is the happiest, Layard sees our agreement on what constitutes the common good as basic. The policies he recommends (which serve as a compendium of policies directed toward the common good) are those that recognize the social nature of human beings and that foster trust and recognize our desire for stability. Being status conscious, human beings must have limits that restrain this feature and policies that recognize the adaptability of humankind. "Happiness depends on your inner life as much as on your outer circumstances," believes Layard. "Thus, public policy can more easily remove misery than augment happiness." The specific policies he recommends focus on developing happiness, readjusting taxes, adopting performance-related pay, and restraining mobility.[2]

Perhaps it is so commonsensical that I shouldn't be surprised by Layard's claim that governmental and social policies are more successful at preventing misery and poor living conditions than they are at positively augmenting our happiness. Nevertheless, this is a helpful reminder that the third sector of society (culture, rather than politics or economics) has much to do with happiness. It is also in keeping with our understanding of the relationship in the United States and other affluent countries between voluntary associations (including the church) and the state. So perhaps we should look to voluntary associations and other means of cultural education and formation to complement governmental policies that assuage misery and foster cultural norms that make for the well-being of all.

We do have some evidence that suggests that generosity contributes to subjective well-being or happiness. In a literature survey and experiment report, James Konow and Joseph Earley of Loyola Marymount University in Los Angeles focus on precisely this question. They find a favorable correlation between generosity and several measures of happiness. "The evidence" from their experiment, they write, "indicates that a tertiary personality variable, sometimes called psychological well-being, is the primary cause of both happiness and greater generosity."[3]

Konow and Earley offer us an interesting metaphor in explaining what "psychological well-being" entails. They ask us to think of it as "a *stock*, similar to the 'hedonic capital' of Graham and Oswald (2006), that produces the *flow* of subjective well-being. Individuals can contribute to this stock by certain types of behavior, including acts of generosity. Higher stocks of psychological well-being are associated with more generous personalities. . . . Thus, generosity is both a long run cause of psychological well-being through repeated acts, as well as a short run effect as with a generous act observed at a given time."[4]

This suggests the importance that economic resources might have to encourage generous activities that promote happiness. Giving produces happiness. Perhaps the happiness line has been flat (the same proportion of affluent Americans have been reporting that they are "very happy" for the past thirty years) because it is a representation of that proportion of the affluent who have contributed some of their resources, indicating that giving has produced happiness. For example, according to sociologists Peggy Thoits and Lyndi Hewitt, volunteer work improves happiness, life satisfaction, self-esteem, and even physical health.[5] Similarly, the *Christian Century* reports that people who did volunteer work were 43 percent more likely to be happy than those who did not. In addition, "people who give money to charity were 43 percent more likely than nongivers to say they are 'very happy' with their lives, according to the Social Capital Community Benchmark Survey. . . . A separate study at the University of Michigan found that people who gave money away were 68 percent less likely to say they had felt hopeless in the past month."[6]

Konow and Earley discuss the implications of their own and other studies. They raise the question of whether greater attention should be paid to the potential benefits of policies that promote charitable donations, volunteerism, service education, and, more generally, community involvement, political action, and social institutions that foster psychological well-being. Konow and Earley's research is especially interesting in light of our earlier discussion about the methodological deficiencies of happiness studies. It points toward what it cannot name—in short, the way that we are inextricably cultural and social, relational all the way down. In short, happiness—no, well-being—is a function of something deeper. Human personhood emerges out of a continuing dynamic energy that operates only through interrelatedness, through a matrix of relations. We exist only through culture understood as the sum total of human interaction. This begins to explain why complicity violates who we are, and why it is destructive of well-being.

Theological perspective: Living God-infused

If Konow and Earley's findings (as well as those of other happiness researchers) are correct, then that suggests corroboration with our theological vision. Past chapters have begun to define that spiritual vision, which is Christian but shares many facets in common with other religious faiths. A central aspect of that faith is that we are interdependent with all other life on this planet. *Shalom.* That interconnection is deep rather than merely utilitarian, though it is that as well. We are defined by each other and by the whole. Moreover, we are constituted by the whole ecosphere. How? Simply consider our dependence on air. Human beings can live five minutes without air, five days without water, and five weeks without food. But rather than stress functionality, let me suggest that this is an internal and constitutional spiritual relationship. We are God-infused. God relates to us. The Spirit dwells within us as well as within others.

If that is true, how did we get to where we are? How did we go wrong? Theologians speak of sin and evil, the ways in which we violate our relationship with God and relationships with others. There are any number of understandings of sin, but for our purpose in this book, the most helpful, I believe, is that sin is a disorder, a falling away from health. It is to fail to be who we were created to be. Sin is not a topic that we like to hear about. The way we choose to ignore our individual sinfulness and our corporate sinfulness in itself may be indicative of the degree to which we are disordered. It is our complicity.

Sin and finitude are part of the actuality of the world, and we human beings have a responsibility to minimize sin and live more and more in such a way that God's intended order becomes our order. Part of what I have been doing throughout this book is to argue that living according to the theological and moral order that we have described will produce the greatest degree of wholeness or completeness possible for us. Not living according to that order produces ill health and despair. That is true because what we have been describing is who we human beings were actually created to be, and we retain the image of God that both constitutes us and also makes for human wholeness.

Our understanding of sin, then, is as a disorderedness that keeps us from who we were meant to be. It involves those barriers that block our becoming the men and women God intends us to be, that keep us from fully enjoying the goodness of this world: food, friends, and family. It is the failure to accept the good, though limited, beings whom we are that leads to sin and unhappiness.

The theological ethicist Charles Mathewes is especially helpful in thinking about the religion of consumption and how it contributes to our ill health, our disorderedness. The claim that we are God-infused and yet live disordered, sinful lives can be connected with Mathewes' argument that uncovers why the ethics of consumption is counterproductive; that is, why it keeps us from our own higher good, our well-being. Mathewes claims that our problem is "not that we remain too religious, but that we are not religious, not 'otherworldly,' enough; we have come to our sorry state by expecting all our needs to be met by and in the world. The solution to our crisis is to care about the world not less, but in a different way than we do."[7] In terms of what I am claiming, then, we live as though we are not God-infused. We live in contradiction to who we are, and thus we block our own well-being.

We have come to a place where we are defining ourselves by our consumption, our desires for consumables. This is not a self-conscious or self-determined process, but one that has seeped into our lives and has made a real (that is to say, not easily reversible) difference. "The increasing capacity of modernity to produce consumer goods has led to a deepening addiction to titillation in the psyches of modern consumers, which has in turn more tightly focused human activities around the pursuit of material goods, both directly—by fostering a deepening consumerist attitude about the world—and indirectly—by altering our moral understandings in certain significant ways."[8] In short, we no longer understand ourselves in ways that transcend our desires.

Insofar as we attempt to meet the material desires that have been generated and that we have adopted, we must expect that we will be consigning ourselves to a perpetual journey without satisfaction. Indeed, the terms of the journey itself preclude lasting satisfaction. We will continue to be hungry ghosts, always seeking and always being disappointed. Rather than rail against the world, we need to learn to love the world more deeply, more religiously. That importantly includes loving other beings who stand under threat or whose lives are miserable. To realize that we are in fact children of God and that we can affirm the world allows us to affirm ourselves, others, and the rest of nature. By understanding who we are as children of the transcendent God who loves, gives, and forgives, we can escape materialistic reduction and a short-circuited well-being. We can do this by acknowledging that our ends transcend any worldly satisfaction; they are directed by our lives in this world toward a transcendent God beyond.

This vision has implications for the meaning of our possessions. What does private ownership (and hence appropriation) mean in light of this divine economy? John Chrysostom proposed that the goal of private ownership was the sharing of the common life of *shalom*. It is the poor, he said, who will stand with us before God on the judgment day. "God has given you many things to possess, not in order that you may use them up for fornication, drunkenness, gluttony, costly clothes, and other forms of soft living, but in order that you may distribute them, to the needy." According to John Chrysostom, we ought to share in the providence of God, who makes the rain to fall on the just and unjust. "Rich and poor alike enjoy the splendid ornaments of the universe. . . . Hence it is said of those who join house to house and estate to estate: 'Shall you alone dwell [You shall dwell alone] in the midst of the earth.' (Isaiah 5:8) The house of the Lord is common to rich and poor."[9] John Calvin, in the same vein, could speak of wages as a "means of grace" for sharing with others. He did this in part because of his understanding of the interdependent community that God fashioned.

Ambrose, the bishop of Milan, lived in a situation where the wealthy were concentrating their land holdings at the expense of smaller peasant farmers. This occasioned Ambrose to cite the same verse from Isaiah to warn of the dangers of subordinating others. He held that ultimately the earth belongs to all of us, "so that the distribution of one's wealth to those in need is a way of returning a trust. Giving to the poor is not a matter of personal whim or inclination; rather, it is necessary and essential to our ownership."[10] Ambrose believed that the offense of the rich lay especially in their isolating themselves from relationship with others.

In short, the right to ownership is not an absolute right in the Christian tradition. The tradition of stewardship holds that we are stewards of God's possessions and have the right of careful use only. Theologian Kathryn Tanner follows a similar line of argument, writing, "This common possession right," based on the norm of the inclusion of all in God's gifting, "means that one should not hold one's property in a primarily exclusive way, guarding it against infringement by others. The right one is exercising to enjoy one's life and livelihood is what is to be shared with all others and not held against them or withheld from them. Your concern is not so much to keep others from what you have, as to see to it that everyone is enjoying what you are [and have]."[11]

In terms of the rich and powerful (or only relatively rich and powerful), what this suggests is that the appropriation of benefits that come at others' expense is a grave danger to ourselves. In effect, by withholding what others need to live, we are violating God's design for all. We are treating as private property what God intended for the use of all. There is not a strict egalitarianism here for the simple reason that we are finite and diverse. Nevertheless, the minimum standard that can be extrapolated from these theological beliefs is that everyone (and every species) is intended to flourish. God wills that all enjoy God's gifts to them. At the very least, we Christians should see to it that all people have what God intended; this certainly entails adequate food, shelter, and health care. In light of these beliefs, world hunger is a scandal of major proportions.

Malnutrition and starvation are indicators of poverty, which almost inevitably implies susceptibility to disease, poor housing, and fragile living conditions. The head of the United Nations food agency reports that some 18,000 children die every day because of hunger and malnutrition and 850 million people go to bed every night with empty stomachs; this a terrible indictment of the world in 2009. I suspect this makes God weep.

Turning to what it might mean positively to adopt the vision of God's giving to all, we can begin by noting that God seems to have had in mind a communal system of cooperation. While we cannot give back to God what God has already given to us, we do offer up our practices and our lives in gratitude, in *eucharista*. We can direct our gifts to God by directing them to God's creatures; we can properly return to God what benefits others and the creation. This furthers the creatures' own good. By holding all things as common in God, we recognize, alongside John Chrysostom, Calvin, and Ambrose, that what we have is a gift and only approximately ours, ours in common. By sharing the hospitality of food with others and also receiving from others, we emulate a system of gift-giving rather than one of exchange or commerce.

What this implies for the acts of giving and receiving is especially inspiring, I think. If we believe that it entails a non-competitive system or economy, as Kathryn Tanner proposes, then it is clear that the lines between what is mine and what is yours are going to get blurred. Calling this principle that of "noncompetition in a community of mutual benefit," Tanner states that the hope for such an economy "gains support when the economic logic of a community dedicated to addressing the needs of all is further specified by a principle of noncompetitive relations that God's gift-giving abides by. So specified, unconditional giving in human relations to meet the needs of all takes on the shape of a community of mutual fulfillment."[12]

In conversation with some African moral theologians, I heard them suggest that some are relatively rich in some respects but poor in others and that the same ones who are poor in some ways are rich in others. The roles of giver and receiver then could properly shift back and forth depending on the situation and need. Through the formation of communities of common property (such as skills, capacities, money, and spiritual maturity), what is needed for the enrichment of all is more likely to be present. We are each more likely to be fulfilled. In other words, my enjoyment of what I have and give to others grows as theirs does. Identifying with others in a joint pursuit of universal benefit. Those who are rich should consider the poverty that others suffer to be something that is happening to them. The letter of Paul to the Corinthians suggests something of the same thing: "If one member suffers, all suffer together with it; if one member is honored, all rejoice together with it" (1 Cor. 12:26). The point of identifying so closely with the poverty of others is to make the good things one has richly the property of those who are without, thus alleviating their poverty. The lives of the poor are to be materially transformed by their being able to draw upon, as their very own property, what one continues to enjoy.

To illustrate, my friend Jerry has an unbelievable ability to be open and honest in addressing such spiritual crises as anger, resentment, jealousy, and consumerism. He has a richness of psychological insight and depth that enables me to raise any question and share any concerns with him. He is very generous in giving me his questions and insights and friendship. I in turn have a wealth of ability to question and critique and offer Jerry honest feedback without offending him in debilitating ways. To be sure, those gifts in which we each are rich can be shared without diminution or loss. As a matter of fact, in contrast, as we use them in common, they are strengthened and refined in each of us.

We who are the rich often see ourselves as givers and not receivers. But God's giving is never done and God's gifts are never separate from the source of the giving, so we are all recipients. If we are all equally dependent on God and can never lock away our possessions, then the playing field between the recipient and the giver, between the poor and the rich, is pretty level.

We have what we have only in relationship with God and with others. Thus, what we own and have is only relatively our own; when we share our gifts, they multiply or diminish as our relationships multiply or diminish. Perhaps that is why Ambrose thought the real danger was in isolating ourselves from others. Having all that we have should not come at the expense of other people. Neither should the noncompetitive community of mutual benefit be one in which the wealthy have their money or capabilities nationalized away from them. This is not a system in which some are winners and some are losers (difficult as it is not to think this way), but instead, one in which all gain by sharing themselves with others.

There is a final relationship that we have incorporated so thoroughly that we might overlook it. That is our relationship to God, which is not reducible to our relationship with others and all natural beings. We yearn for a relationship with the transcendent Giver who guarantees our lives. We want to so incorporate into our lives the God who grounds our being that we continually live more and more as we were intended to live—joyfully. From this perspective we also see that God's law is a gracious law; it is a guide to living well and is in harmony with who we essentially are.

Jesus summed up the law in two commandments: love your neighbor as yourself, we remember, but the first commandment is to love God with all your heart, mind, and soul (see Matt. 22:37-39). We forget that commandment to our peril. The peril is that, by allowing our definition of what we owe our neighbor, ourselves, and the earth to float free of its anchor in the first commandment, we lose sight of just what it is that makes us human and why we should love our neighbor and the earth. At least that is what Christians believe. Without a foundation in the first commandment, our definition of what constitutes good for neighbor, self, and earth may go awry. Thus, it is significant to ask what it means to love God.

Two elements constitute this love. They are parallel to the commandments and offer a comprehensive overview. The first is that we owe God our worship as Creator, Sustainer, and Redeemer. This is first a religious response to the love of God; our adoration and praise of God flow from our gratitude and our astonishment at God's grace. But if it is truly worship, then it will influence (if not determine) the rest of our lives, including our moral life. It will shape who we are, what we do, and who we become.

Second, our impulse will be to love God with all our being. We will seek to give back in response to God's giving. While this is a basic and defining sentiment, we cannot reciprocate to God. The closest we come to sharing with God is to share with the remainder of the creation. The best we can do, and what God wants us to do, is to love others and all creation, including ourselves. God wills that we delight in him and also share with others. These are the twin responses of worship and sharing with others. The belief in God and in the nature of God makes a huge difference in the ethics that we adopt, since it influences our beliefs about who human beings are. It is not overstating the case to say that the love of God can pervade our lives.

Moral directions: The ethics of consumption versus the ethics of communion

At this point the differences that we have been drawing have become clear. We have been articulating the difference between an ethic of consumption and an ethic of communion. Theologians speak of this in terms of theological anthropology, the doctrine of who human beings are. An ethics of consumption is based on a view of humankind as *homo economicus*—human beings are essentially economic beings who seek to fulfill themselves by achieving a comfortable and challenging lifestyle. The ethics of communion is based on a view of humankind as children of God who find their fulfillment in loving God and neighbor and enjoying their lives. We are contrasting the ethic of consumption that is tied to appropriation in our global economy to an ethic of communion or covenant with God. Without an understanding of God or at least of a transcendent good, we would not be able to see that consumption is a secondary value and not in the governing position.

God entered into communion with us on the basis of God's own delight in the creation and yearning to be in relationship with us. God's grace is sovereign and comes before any otherworldly concern. Thus, one form of Reformed ethic is that of obedience to God and God's law, which the Reformed tradition understands as a form of the gospel. We are to regard the wellbeing of our neighbor as our own; the law expresses God's intentions for how we are to treat our neighbor and the earth. We are to be stewards, to enjoy the material world but not worship it or make it an idol. From this perspective, a critique of consumerism would illumine the ways it is (or can be) idolatrous.

Another form of ethics in the Christian tradition stresses the moral life as our response to God's freely offered grace, a life lived in gratitude to God. This is a theocentric ethic. We are to live in response to God, not in response to material goods that have a circumscribed place in our lives; they are to be "means of grace," not the end of living. Thinkers such as H. Richard Niebuhr, Jonathan Edwards, and Calvin subscribe to this form of ethic.

A Roman Catholic view of consumerism would develop its critique on the basis of an "anthropological claim about what constitutes the genuinely human and what values and practices serve authentic development," summarizes Professor Kenneth Himes of Boston College. "While not overlooking other forms of criticism such as care for the poor and environmental sustainability, the conviction about what constitutes human well-being is what generates the strongest papal criticism of consumerism."[13]

Thus, we have come to the bedrock question: Why does appropriation matter? We know that many people are dying and we have the means to save them, yet we choose to spend our resources on luxuries. From the perspective of an ethics of consumption, why does that matter? In many ways, though it may be morally repugnant to us, there is no reason except one's individual and fickle sentiment of compassion. There is no transcendent reason that puts consumption in its place and articulates why consumption should take secondary place to others' well-being.

We get a very different answer from the perspective of the ethics of communion. To the question "Why does it matter that many could be saved if we were to reappropriate our luxuries?" the ethics of communion says, "Because they are children of God just as we are." Note that others matter because we believe they are infinitely valuable to God to the same degree that we are. They have done as little to deserve their bad fortune as we have done to deserve our good. We are the disciples to whom Jesus says, "You give them something to eat" (Matt. 14:16). We are concerned about those who are suffering because we have been commissioned to feel their pain as our own.

The ethics of communion understands this not as a matter of charity or compassion or even love and mercy primarily, but as an act of justice and law. The Bible makes this clear in its consistent witness from the gleaning laws to the Jubilee injunctions to

Jesus' teachings and example. Our concern with poverty is not an issue of generosity but of rights. If a rich man knows of someone who is starving and has the power to help that person but chooses not to do so, then he violates the starving person's rights as surely and reprehensibly as if he had physically assaulted the sufferer. Similarly, author and Wartburg Seminary professor Craig Nessan sees the care of the starving as a matter of orthopraxis for which we the affluent will be held accountable.[14]

Notice that we have now given both a religious reason for caring for our neighbor—she or he is a fellow child of God with infinite value to God—and a moral, law-based reason for caring—we have biblical and other laws and ethics that direct us to do this. *Finally, however, what this book has claimed is that we were created in such a way that caring for our neighbor is essential to our well-being.* It is vital to our own happiness as Homo sapiens. It is even in our self-interest. This of course is a truth that is independent of what anyone believes in particular. This is a claim about our psychological, social, and physical makeup. The world is created in such a way that not working to alleviate another's suffering damages our own well-being, especially if we are appropriating the benefits of the others' poor living conditions. Thus, even if one is not a believer, this remains true, if not immediately then ultimately: *What makes for the well-being of others works for one's own well-being. This is not dependent on the response of the other.*

Catholic theologian Monika Hellwig made this claim even more strongly. God built a "foundation of hope" into the very design of creation; the work of forgiveness and grace is built into the world. "It is," wrote Hellwig,

"because the hunger for authentic love is not only a need to receive but a need to be able to give that we have a human base for hope at all. It is because in their true depth the hunger of the starving and the hunger of the (literally) spoilt rich are complementary that we have an urgent need to seek redemption from our false securities, selfishness, exaggerated anxiety over self-preservation."

According to Hellwig, "In the Eucharist we have an answer to despair about the future of the world; we can still live and bid others live because we are drawn into a covenant with God and all humankind within which to give one's life is ultimately to save one's life."[15]

From that perspective it makes sense to see that caring for other children of God is deeply satisfying. Furthermore, it helps us understand our nature and also our destiny. We can give and receive in relationship with others because we know we can only rest in God.

I know that this is the direction in which well-being lies. I believe that. But how to get to a place where I could live that moral life, how to get to a place where I could experience that well-being? Well, that is the pursuit of happiness, isn't it? That is what we all want. So that is what we take up in our last chapter.

Questions for digestion

1. Imagine that the world was arranged in a way that our well-being depended on the well-being of others. How many of our current global problems would violations of that arrangement explain? Would it explain spiritual health and illness? Would it explain why complicity blocks fully experiencing well-being?

2. According to the reports in this chapter, sharing, giving, and volunteering seem positively related to happiness or well-being. What is your personal experience with such activities? Have they affected you positively? How might awareness of this connection affect your future actions?

3. In what ways do we as human beings living in twenty-first-century America "transcend our desires"? How are we more than our desires?

4. Compare the ethics of consumption with the ethics of communion.

6

How Can We Reverse
Complicity and Nourish
Our Souls?

How do rich Christians in the most powerful nation on earth deal with the reality of global poverty? In this last chapter we will set aside our usual format and look at practical ways to reverse acts of appropriation, especially in respect to world hunger and our own insatiability. Asking, "How can we learn to be satisfied?" might be a first step.

The focus here will be on personal and social transformation. This really scares me personally, since I am writing from the comfort of a wonderful office overlooking the Kansas City skyline. I like my creature comforts as much as anyone, I suspect. So I do not underestimate the challenge that the imperative to be transformed presents. But if we are to deal with the threats that consumption presents to our ecological home, to our society, to global peoples, and to you and me personally, we have to face this challenge. Let me note that I believe our own personal happiness and sense of well-being are also at stake.

Facing our realities

We live with appetites unsatisfied, but we live pretty comfortably. It is difficult to modify a way of life that is so materially and physically enjoyable. Indeed, Scripture makes it abundantly clear that God wants us to enjoy ourselves. However, we know that our way of life comes at the cost to the environment and to the lives of many global peoples who live in poverty. Furthermore, it is clear that this cannot go on much longer: the prospect of seven billion people (or more) living as we do simply cannot happen with the resources that are available now.

My argument is that a comfortable standard of living is secondary to the primary good. This is no anti-materialist diatribe, but instead an argument that we have forgotten that we are communal people who live with others. But we have substituted, or sought to substitute, the comfort of good food and good housing and stimulating entertainment for the community of other people. That has happened at great cost to our collective and individual happiness and well-being. Basically no such substitution is possible without consequence.

We need to face the reality that at our core we are relational beings. The reason the realities of world hunger cause a wrenching in our gut is because we are empathetic. Interacting with others is the source of our greatest joy.

As human beings we are also spiritual beings. We seek meaning that transcends our day-to-day lives. We want our lives to have meaning, direction, and hope. We seek to have a relationship with God because we are thoroughly spiritual people. We yearn to be content and to live in worthwhile ways. We know that we are not only creatures of the flesh, but also creatures of the Spirit. We want to incarnate the way of the Spirit, to live on earth as in heaven.

This said, we can face our complicity in appropriation. Indeed, we can only participate in the hopeful work of restoration and reconciliation if we acknowledge our complicity in the systems that have produced hunger and poverty. We are deeply implicated in the state of affairs that requires transformation; the possibility of breaking the patterns described in this book requires facing that reality. It's a process:

Step 1: Awareness and acknowledgment. In order to effect transformation, we must first recognize what our lifestyle is doing and the burdens it is putting on others. There is a contemporary movement that offers us a way out of the dead end of materialistic consumption and helps us to face our reality so that we can begin to go in the direction of relational joy. That way is the focus on practices. A veritable library of materials has been retrieved from Christian tradition and modified within the past two decades.[1] One practice that ties in with the need to face reality and to remember who we are is the practice of self-examination and confession. This practice has functioned to maintain the skill of awareness and self-criticism.

Step 2: Confession and repentance. Two elements are necessary to penitence. The first is the assurance that God will continue to love us and to forgive us our morally troublesome behavior. This point can be made graphically. God enters into friendship with us; thus, Jesus says to his disciples, "I do not call you servants any longer, because the servant does not know what the master is doing; but I have called you friends, because I have made known to you everything I have heard from my Father" (John 15:15). That is the assurance of forgiveness.

The second element is our confidence that there is another way to live that can substitute for the old in a manner that is life enhancing. Part of being a community of "disruptive empathy" is that members of the community *embody* the way of life they recommend. Witnessing to a different truth is far more important than arguing for it. Such communities give us hope that things can be different. So Jesus commands, "Love one another as I have loved you" (John 15:12). This is the basis of the new community of which we are speaking. We in the Christian community affirm that this is the legitimate place of the church. As a global and local presence, the church has the ability to witness to the transformative power of awareness, repentance, and then transformation. Most denominations have hunger programs and support local and global efforts to lift up those in poverty. The church is not simply a private club or service provider. Indeed, it is to be the body of Christ in the world.

Step 3: Transformation (or sanctification). The third step after self-examination, confession, and repentance is transformation. This is a long process that theologians have spoken of as "sanctification." Sanctification is the process of living more and more into the ideal Christian life. Sanctification is in fact movement into well-being; as we become more centered on living out the way of God, we are more fulfilled. This is not a matter of drudgery, but of self-consciously and deliberately disciplining oneself into what turns out to be a joy-filled lifestyle. The ways we practice are transformative.

Changing our eating practices

Since the particular topic on which our attention has focused here is that of world hunger, it is appropriate that we look at Christian practices that have been associated with eating. The contemporary focus on practices has defined them as activities that arise in conjunction with meeting needs that are essential to human life, and certainly eating is one of those. Those practices have the power to change one's life and to alter it in ways that make for enjoyment. There are seven such eating practices: saying grace, feasting, fasting, sharing and offering hospitality, honoring the body, preparing food, and partaking in the Eucharist itself. Many thinkers have recognized the way eating patterns reflect the customs and values of a society, be they Hindu, Muslim, or Jain. As a Christian community, we must strive to retrieve the resource of those practices.

Vincent Miller, associate professor of theology at Georgetown University, has made a disturbingly convincing case that the reigning consumerist mentality affects the way we approach Christian values and beliefs. This is true not only of Christian values and beliefs, but also of other religious, republican, and civic values and beliefs. Miller writes, "Consumer culture is best diagnosed not as a deformation of belief but as a particular way of engaging religious beliefs that divorces them from practice."[2] Consider what it might mean if Miller is correct—that consumerism divorces beliefs from practices—and if religious beliefs without practices are simply a luxury. In short, if we lose the connection between what we say we believe and what we do, we have simply surrendered to the false gospel of consumption.

However, we can retrieve those practices that reintegrate our very selves—that allow us to live with integrity. A successful response will attend to the structures and practices that connect belief to daily life and to the lived, everyday theology of believing communities; thus, it will adopt the task of helping communities preserve and sustain their traditions in the face of the erosion of globalizing capitalism. It's about connecting our actions with consequences.

An eating practice related to penitence, self-examination, and renewal is that of *fasting*, which I have often called the most valuable spiritual practice for our time. Fasting can awaken us to who we are as human creatures. It can alert us to the fact that we have limits, that we are bodily creatures, and that we can live without all that stuff we think we need. In short, it can help us become reintegrated. "In a culture driven by endless shouts of 'More!', fasting can simply be a faithful affirmation of 'Enough!' " writes Christian poet Marilyn Chandler McEntyre.[3] Imagine that—we are only about eighteen hours away from an embodied revelation of who we are *and* of the fact that we can do without all that stuff we carry around! Fasting is an opportunity that is absolutely counter-consumer-cultural and one that can clarify our priorities. Some people do fast in penitence and/or self-examination, and that is all to the good. Others—and I really like this aspect of it—offer the money they would otherwise have spent on food to a hunger relief agency. Fasting helps us break the cycle of appropriation. Perhaps most significantly, fasting teaches us that we can in fact live without needing to seek immediate gratification of every appetite.

A surprising eating practice that teaches us about appropriation is that of honoring the body. What many would see as a matter quite simply of dieting, honoring the body is a set of practices that enables us to dispose of our physical selves in sharing and enjoyable ways. And yet the American way of eating is often a reflection of consumerism—a grab-and-go mentality that fails to appreciate the very self! How ironic can it get! Eating lower on the food chain is in fact eating better. In contrast, our Western diet has (1) increased the rates of cancer, heart disease, diabetes, and obesity; (2) caused immigrants from countries with low rates of these diseases to quickly acquire them;

and (3) generated efforts to understand and solve the problem that have actually made it worse. We can "honor our bodies" and enjoy them as healthy and moderate eaters. Our present market system socializes us into intemperance and overeating. A number of studies have found that Americans overwork; perhaps we live in an intemperate culture that siphons attention and energy primarily into the cycle of labor and consumption, with sad results for nonmarket relations and practices. Eating with temperance suggests the benefits of slowing down, of renouncing our hyperactivity so that we can enjoy our eating, our friends, our families, God.

Practicing sharing and hospitality

In addition to self-examination, fasting, and other eating practices, sharing and hospitality are essential to our renewal, to our movement away from appropriation. In general, rather than promoting generosity and openness, accumulating more and more seems to make one less open and generous.[4] Despite powerful exceptions, accumulation seems to be a self-intensifying negative practice that makes one stingier and stingier. But the good news is that sharing and hospitality tend to be self-intensifying as well. Once we begin to share with others, we get bitten by the bug and find this enormously satisfying. How many times have you heard people who have volunteered to work in shelters or food kitchens or who have returned from mission trips say, "I received so much more than I gave." That is simply true! The line between giving and receiving is a thin one; in fact, it is almost as though the practices are linked—giving-receiving. This should not surprise us. In fact, we were made to share. Sharing makes us happy, because we are sharing creatures. I suspect that the people in this country who call themselves "very happy" are those who have learned sharing and hospitality.

Appropriation of others' time, energy, and life-chances is very much opposed to what gives life. If one thinks of the example of Jesus (or the Buddha, or Francis of Assisi, or all manner of other saints), then it is clear how very far appropriation is from the beings we were created to be. One practice that can break the stranglehold of consumerism is that of tithing (a form of sharing and hospitality). Giving away a tenth of one's income in a society that encourages spending into indebtedness is not only a challenge to revise our consumer patterns but also teaches us that we are accountable before God for what we have and what we do with it. In the same way that fasting helps us discover that we are dependent on God for daily bread, sharing shows us the satisfaction that comes with passing on some of the gifts that God has given us.

Living more corporately

What we can do to reverse the fact of appropriation as individuals is important to our own well-being and to the well-being of those who benefit from our acts of reappropriation. For years we have been bombarded with advertisements and other allurements that have led us into appropriation. We have learned some habits of consumption and automatic practice. We need some practical steps toward reversing the impact of our cheap food policies. This section, then, offers a set of opportunities toward greater well-being. When people change, that change happens either (1) by our realizing that present patterns are not working well; (2) by crisis and (at least to some extent) forced change; or (3) by positive engagement. Let's consider all three.

1. Being discontent with present patterns

One step on the way to change is simply coming to a greater awareness of our own discontent with our present patterns. If we are alert to the fact that our lifestyle is not producing the happiness it promised or if we feel as though something is missing or that somehow life is a bit empty, then we may be led to experiment with something different. One of those "things" that many people find satisfying these days is church mission trips to areas where help is needed. A dramatic example is the outpouring of mission trips to the Gulf Coast after Hurricanes Katrina and Rita in the fall of 2005 that continues to this day. It's exciting to see community service and embodied pedagogy built into church programming in a way that shows that such volunteering is not optional or just a whim, but is at the center of learning and living.

In a review of recent research on volunteering, a growing body of evidence indicates that volunteering provides individual health benefits in addition to social benefits. There is a strong relationship between volunteering and health; those who volunteer have lower mortality rates, greater functional ability, and lower rates of depression later in life than those who do not volunteer. Especially striking are the benefits for those who volunteer more than one hundred hours a year and for older volunteers. Opportunities to do such work are as close as your computer or your pastor or your newspaper. Virtually every city or town in the country has a food bank or food pantry that one can work in and contribute to. My own experience has been that being on-site, meeting people who are different from me, and talking to them is invaluable. There is no substitute for it.

Other people seeking a change in life have become so fed up with "the system" that they drop off the grid entirely. These are people who have decided that the present pattern of working sixty, seventy, eighty hours a week is simply no way to live. They have decided to find ways of making a living and enjoying life that do not consume their free time or take them away from spouse, children, family, and/or friends. Among those who have changed their patterns recently are two of my favorite authors, Barbara Kingsolver and Bill McKibben. Both (independently as far as I know) decided to depend for one year on food that had been locally grown. Their experiments are reported in Kingsolver's *Animal, Vegetable, Miracle: A Year of Food Life* and McKibben's *Deep Economy: The Wealth of Communities and the Durable Future*.[5] Most telling to me is their sheer joy in growing their own food.

Moreover, it would be helpful to break out of our provincialism in addressing the issue of appropriation; we could become more aware of how other peoples live. Close to a billion people are living at the one-dollar-a-day level, and we simply cannot imagine that. The situation in Darfur and other countries reminds us that the world continues to allow thirty thousand children to die every day of poverty. Maybe the cause is indifference, and that indifference is born from a lack of firsthand experience. Undergraduates are not required to learn how the global majority lives, though there are encouraging signs that that is changing. My recommendation is simply to become more educated about how other peoples are living and to experience that if possible. Perhaps people whose perspectives are not privileged but a bit on the margin—such as ethnic minorities, poor persons, women, members of the GLBTQ community, or refugees—can help us understand what hunger is. Spending time living with people who may be different from us would help us realize that Jesus died for them and that they are our brothers and sisters in God.

Another suggestion would be to watch less television. Television has been called "the throbbing heart of the monster called consumerism." Studies have shown the impact of television on making us obese, noting that the two best predictors of obesity are income level and the amount of television one watches a day. The latter is especially the case for children. Moreover, watching television has the impact of lulling us into believing that all people have a decent level of income and that things always turn out okay at the end of the show. It narcotizes us to the plight of others. Furthermore, there is some evidence that the more television one watches, the more one becomes dissatisfied with one's own life and also thinks the world is a place to be feared and other people not trusted. Do you detect a spiritual problem here that relates to appropriation?

To summarize this section on the way to get started by changing our patterns, we could:

1. volunteer to help others;
2. grow some portion of our food each year;
3. learn more about (or better, experience) how other global peoples are living; and
4. watch less television.

2. Changing through crisis

Another way people change is through crisis, and I believe that we could learn about appropriation in this way. We simply cannot continue to live the way we have been in the wake of crisis. When something catastrophic happens, change is forced upon us. One thing that may cause people to change their ways is disease. Our affluent lifestyle contributes to its share of mental, spiritual, and physical illnesses. The American diet, as has been pointed out, causes many diseases and necessitates a multi-billion-dollar health industry. Doctors will tell us when diagnosing morbid obesity or heart disease that unless we change our habits, we will continue to experience a greatly diminished quality of life. The same goes for diabetes and respiratory illness. I just don't know a better example of the problem of having too much than these illnesses.

It's also time to rethink the notion that more stuff makes people happier. Once found to have the happiest people in the world, the United States now ranks twenty-third. Alcoholism, suicide, and depression rates have soared, with fewer than one in three Americans claiming to be very happy. "All that material progress—and all the billions of barrels of oil and million of acres of trees that it took to create it—seems not to have moved the satisfaction meter an inch," writes Bill McKibben. "It's as if we've done an experiment in whether consumption produces happiness and determined that it doesn't."[6]

Another form of crisis that can cause change is environmental. The planet simply cannot afford the increased demands that come with a Western culture and lifestyle that is rapidly spreading to densely populated countries such as China and India. We are at an opportune time of decision-making, a point that has the potential to dramatically reconfigure the planet and our food and energy supply. In effect, we are two nations: (1) Wal-Mart Nation (gigantic, globalized, unsustainable in the face of climate change and the trashing of nature and the coming exhaustion of the world's fossil fuels) and (2) Farmers' Market Nation (manageably small, localized, communitarian, neighborly, calibrated to the human scale).

There continues to be a worldwide food crisis in which many are not able to get the bare subsistence that they were used to. While there are many culprits to blame, one thing that is clear is that Western nations are using grain to feed cattle and make biofuel while others go hungry. Many organizations are addressing this crisis and making admirable attempts to ensure that development efforts accompany the relief of immediate need.

To summarize these steps in working toward transformation, we could:

1. learn to eat more healthily and to share;
2. become even more conscious of our environmental footprint; and
3. join a group that is combating world hunger.

3. Engaging in life-giving activities

The way to change that I like best is through positive engagement, through our realization of more enjoyable directions. We have hinted at some already: helping others can really contribute to a sense of well-being; growing your own food (even some of it) can be an extremely enjoyable experience; and living more simply in general can have enormous rewards.

One of the life-giving activities that is especially engaging and is central to our well-being is intimacy with others. As my friend Russ puts it, "You can't hug your BMW." If we were created for relationship and relating to others is part of our constitution, then being in genuine community with others is essential to well-being. While we may empathize with others' suffering, too often we want to avoid it. But we actually cheat ourselves by "not wanting to get involved" when that very involvement, that sharing, would be a time of intimacy that could feed us. The feeling we would discover through our involvement is compassion. If we are the one suffering, we might have the grace to see that asking others to share the suffering (maybe just to the extent of listening to our situation) can be a way of giving them a gift. Praying with others and simply being present can combat fear and hopelessness. Listening to others and being alert to them can be a receiving experience as well. Rather than learning to squelch compassion, we can discover that listening to and sharing with others are engaging and enjoyable experiences.

Another practice is modeled by many people living lower on the food chain. The way in which we are attracted to those who are content and happy flies in the face of our own drive to "get ours." The saints of the church are attractive to us because we desire for ourselves the lives of peace and profound well-being they exhibit. So the Dali Lama is a role model for many because he lives simply, seems to have a deep well of assurance and to live with spiritual calmness. He seems to have a deep trust that drives out fear. Francis of Assisi continues to be a model for many of us in his love for all nature and all people, because he denounced wealth (as did the Buddha) and lived a life of great faith. We are attracted to the notion of living simply and within our means and also within a pattern of familial contentment.

We are attracted as well to the Bill and Melinda Gates and Warren Buffets of this world who want to "give back" a portion of what they have accumulated. That desire to "give back" is at the heart of Christian stewardship and is part of what engages us to reverse appropriation. We can appreciate good modeling and strive to emulate the virtues of generosity and reciprocity.

Another engaging practice is simply becoming grateful for all that we have received. We may desire to give back to God in worship a portion of what we have so much enjoyed. The impulse to gratitude and generosity is such a wonderful, almost inexpressible feeling that it overflows into giving on to others. This impulse is one that we could give greater license to. Many of us have been taught to live out of a scarcity mentality, but living out of abundance is much more enjoyable and holistically captivating. Maybe then we could see that the affluent also need our sharing and they could learn to share themselves.

These people are attractive to us in part because they seem to have come to appreciate what is and what we have. It is a way of stopping and enjoying rather than feeling the need to keep moving on to the next achievement or acquisition. Financial planner Penny Lauritzen reminds us that we can imagine that we are in a long line ranging from the poorest to the richest. We will always be somewhere in the middle. "What is important is the direction I choose to look and walk. . . . If I am always looking to the wealthy end, I am going to think I am poor and feel I need more. But if I work on turning myself around to look, though sometimes scary, in the opposite direction to those who have less, my life can be transformed. Values of community, sharing, gratitude and relationship will become more the focus of my life."[7] So long as we keep looking at the richest, we will fail to enjoy what we do have. But if we look in the opposite direction, we see that we can share and be a part of others. We have a need to say thanks, to be grateful, and to live graciously. That is true enjoyment.

To sum up, taking the first step can be as simple as:

1. attending to our relationships with others;
2. following the patterns of those who live contented lives; and
3. living and giving out of our abundance.

Participating in life-giving organizations

An essential aspect of relieving the hunger and misery of the poor is corporate change. Our wealth does create impoverishment, and organized policy changes and action will be needed to reverse this trend. We benefit from a political economy that exploits and oppresses many of the world's people; thus, we are responsible for transforming the structures of power that cause that oppression. Holding ourselves accountable to all those people from whose labor and poverty we benefit may be the most vital challenge of the twenty-first century. Such actions will become increasingly urgent because of climate change and worldwide hunger. As Christians, we are obliged to serve the cause of justice and compassion. We must find a way of being corporately responsible. One way is to act through organizations to transform economic corporations and political systems to benefit the poor. And in so doing we can increase our own sense of well-being as well.

Social entrepreneurship

Two of the organizations grouped under this category are well known; perhaps the best is the Grameen Bank efforts of Muhammad Yunus who started by making loans of 62 cents on average and now has reached 100 million clients in 100 countries. That effort is even profitable financially. Other efforts include the Institute for Liberty and Democracy in Peru, El Salvador, Egypt, Mexico, and other nations, which gives poor people title to their own land. Other efforts include paying poor mothers to send their children to school and health clinics and linking villages by roads that enable people to sell produce and bring in needed inputs.

One of the most expansive efforts is kiva.org. Working through the Internet, even moderately well-off people can make loans (as low as $25) around the world to entrepreneurs who are making the effort to get out of poverty and feed their children. This is a remarkable organization that reinforces my desire to be partners with people in Cote d'Ivoire, Guatemala, and Pakistan. So far, my loans have been paid off and I have been delighted to reinvest in other people's initiative and self-development.

Lobbying and relief efforts

Another way to advocate change is by supporting the efforts of organizations that bring direct relief to those who are suffering and of those who lobby for positive public policy. Some organizations' persistence and conscientiousness have resulted in admirable efforts around the world, including Bread for the World (bread.org); the Foods Resource Bank (foodsresourcebank.org); Heifer International (heifer.org); Oxfam International (Oxfam. org); and all the denominational hunger programs and local church efforts. These organizations work to strengthen local self-help groups internationally, they encourage global development efforts to feed hungry people, and some also provide emergency relief. They usually have a lobbying arm as well. In almost every community, we can find such organizations hard at work; they would be glad to have us join them.

Local foods movement

Let me just tell you about one aspect of the local foods movement, and that is my Food Policy Council in Kansas City. Addressing issues of malnutrition, poverty, and education, this coalition has attracted an assortment: public school personnel, people from the community gardening movement, government officials, social agency and hospital representatives, and other civic-minded people. My point is that this local foods movement has attracted a lot of attention and action in many cities (kchealthykids.org).

Governmental policy

Finally, there is the area of governmental policy, which will be important to the mobilization of individuals and organizations. President Obama can tackle many of the issues that defined his campaign—energy policy, public health, and climate change—by considering the reorganization of the food system in this country.

Enormous savings in energy and pollution and health care can be realized by weaning the citizens of affluent nations from fossil fuel onto solar and wind fuel. Most of the problems associated with the food system have to do with our reliance on oil. Present policy resists this conversion and produces food that is not nutritious in the process. While producing a bushel of grain requires a half gallon of oil, grass can be grown with little more than sunshine. There may be real savings in the level of subsidies we pay to corporate producers, as well as results that are healthier for boys and girls.

The food system needs to become more regional. Rather than a global or national system where we wind up shipping the same foods east and west, and burning a lot of fuel to transport these foods in the process, we the consumers need a more diversified food system, one that is more imaginative and shortens the food chain. The local food movement is well aware of the benefits of this already; food grown locally is healthier, less expensive, and requires less processing. Farmers' markets, community-supported farms, locavore restaurants, and creative cookery all point in this direction. There is much federal policy that could support this movement: agriculture enterprise zones, four seasons farmers' markets, local food inspection, and many other such steps could make us far more self-dependent, in terms of both fuel and health care expenses.

In order to solve the food crisis, we need to fix the food system. Governmental policies can reregulate the market, reduce the oliogopolistic power of the agri-foods corporations, and rebuild local agroecologically resilient family agriculture. According to Eric Holt-Gimenez of the Food First Organization, "We need to make food affordable by turning the food system into an engine for local economic development in both rural and urban areas."[8] We can make food affordable, the marketing of food fair, and farming viable once again. We can do these things together.

The price and availability of safe and secure food are rapidly becoming an issue. Internationally the lack of safe food or any food at all has diplomatic and military ramifications that are exacerbated by the reality of climate change and the intensification of flooding in a number of already-unstable parts of the world. The diet of our children and of poor people would benefit from the encouragement of fruit and vegetable production and the redirection of subsidies away from those who produce unhealthy products (corn fructose, for example). The reeducation of the American people will be important to their health, to the lowering of the energy we spend on food production and transportation, and to the well-being of the environment, of which we are a part.

To sum up, we can make big changes with small steps, such as:

1. making small loans to help encourage social entrepreneurship;
2. supporting relief organizations and hunger lobbying efforts;
3. encouraging the local foods movement; and
4. working to change government policy by writing to our legislators, reeducating ourselves, and getting involved in the political process.

Questions for digestion

1. What keeps you from letting go of "things" in order to focus on the needs of others? How do you think changing your focus might affect your life?
2. Do you agree with the statement that we must do with less in order for all to have more? What does that mean for you personally?
3. Has a crisis ever effected change in your life? What was the result?
4. In what ways have you supported organizations that seek to help those who are poor and hungry? Are you comfortable with attempting change by working with governmental policy? Why or why not?

CONCLUSION

I hope that you have been able to feel that there is light at the end of our journey of recognition. There is relief from the gloom of appropriation and there is hope for a brighter physical and spiritual well-being. While the issue of complicity is complicated, we have experienced plenty of good news—gospel—as we have journeyed together. So I think an apt conclusion to our discussion comes from the Gospels—the story about Zacchaeus from the Gospel of Luke (Luke 19:1-10).

You remember Zacchaeus, I suspect. He was a man "short of stature" who wanted to see the celebrity Jesus as he came through town. So this tax collector, who may have been short on character as well as on height, climbed a sycamore tree. When Jesus got to where Zacchaeus was, he looked up and said, "Zacchaeus, come down; today I am going to eat with you." (Jesus doesn't ask for an invitation!)

What is interesting about Zacchaeus's response is this: When Jesus came in the door, Zacchaeus recognized the evil of his ways. (Tax collectors were notorious for greed and corruption.) Immediately he repented of his evil and told Jesus that he would give half of what he owned to the poor and would make four-fold restitution to those he had defrauded.

The words he received from Jesus are those we also need: "Today healing has come to this house." *Soteria* has come to this house—salvation, healing.

I suspect that that is what we are looking for—healing, wholeness, purpose, a sense of worthwhileness in our lives, a sense that our work is blessed. We want well-being, well-being beyond happiness. Corporate well-being.

The good news—the gospel—is that this is possible. Jesus wants to eat with us, too. We can be transformed, but only on the basis of forgiveness. And it can be intimated that such transformation and well-being are best achieved through being with the hungry, the food insecure, and those who need the basic necessities of life. The reason Henri Nouwen and Jean Vanier were such happy people is because they worked with the poor and mentally ill every day. They were able to see and receive the blessing of being in *communio*. They were in the presence of God.

In case all this is sounding too pious, let me remind you of the research we reviewed on the sources of unhappiness and of happiness. It is becoming pretty clear that hoarding and keeping (to say nothing of "taking") are not going to make you or me happy. Time and time again, report after report suggests that those who are happiest are those who are working to make life better for others, such as those who volunteer or work in helping professions. The reason they are happy, I suspect, has to do with what they receive from their giving.

There are many opportunities for us to assuage the complicity that creeps into our bones. Let no one suggest that I think this is easy; it is not. I have been much impressed with the work of philosopher Judith Butler, who argues that we are born into social structures that we did not make, and we must be humble about the degree to which we can change them or change even our own conduct. But if you belong to a community of good-will, I really believe you can begin to roll back the forces of appropriation.

I would love to find a way to discover how we can recognize the difference we are making. Perhaps as a start, we just need to talk about it. We need to tell each other how we see food pantries, church outreach activities, hunger relief agencies, fair trade groups working to help others. We might discuss how the present recession impacts our sense of appropriation and our response to it.

Maybe today we are in the place of the rich man who came to see Jesus (Mark 10:17-27). His question was basically "What must I do to be saved, to be healed?" Jesus asked him to sell all he had and give to the poor and follow him. The Bible reports that "he was shocked and went away grieving, for he had many possessions" (v. 22). Apparently he didn't like Jesus' prescription. But as we have seen, his healing and the healing of the suffering are connected. The key to the rich man's healing (the complicit man's healing) is to be found in redressing the economic imbalance, the injustice done to the poor. But more than that, Jesus' words may be showing us that our own excess of stuff is suffocating us. We are trapped in a system that promises to heal us. But our experience is that, however comfortable our lives are, they still lack something.

Perhaps it is comfort that disguises from us the real disease of appropriation that we—with God's help—need to treat. We can address the hunger of the world. There is a way of life that makes for profound well-being. We have been forgiven, and our greatest joy is to treat our brothers and sisters as the children of God they are. That is the path beyond complicity to joy.

NOTES

Introduction

1. "Islam Solves World Poverty and Hunger," www.al-islami. com/islam/islam_poverty.php (accessed September 29, 2007). *Zakat* means both "purification" and "growth," suggesting that setting aside a portion of our wealth for the hungry purifies our wealth and makes for our growth.

2. See Barbara Kingsolver, *Animal, Vegetable, Miracle: A Year of Food Life* (New York: HarperCollins, 2007); Michael Pollan, *In Defense of Food: An Eater's Manifesto* (New York: Penguin, 2008); and Alice Waters, *The Art of Simple Food: Notes, Lessons, and Recipes from a Delicious Revolution* (New York: Crown Publishing, 2007) for examples of contemporary humanistic authors who highlight the moral values in the food-related choices we make.

3. Complicity, in distinction from guilt, is associated with enjoying the benefits of the actions that bring suffering or miserable living conditions to others. It is indirect, not intended, but assists however incrementally in the support of an unjust system. It is the appropriation of benefits produced unjustly. Sometimes it is labeled "the sweatshop issue."

4. This is my third book about the spiritual and moral meaning of food. The two former books point to this one. The first, *Food for Life: The Spirituality and Ethics of Eating* (Minneapolis: Fortress

Press, 2004), was a hunting expedition to track down exactly what the Christian tradition had to say about food. What I found was that the global food supply system violates God's intentions that everyone delight in eating and learn to share food with other people. The second book, *Sharing Food: Christian Practices for Enjoyment* (Minneapolis: Fortress Press, 2006), sought to retrieve and revive some historic eating practices—seven of them, to be exact. Some of these are explicitly Christian—partaking in Eucharist, saying grace—but others are not, such as preparing food and honoring the body through exercise and diet. Not only are these practices healthy; they embody delight and sharing, community and hospitality.

5. Thomas Pogge, "Severe Poverty as a Violation of Negative Duties," *Ethics and International Affairs* 19, no. 1 (2005): 81.

6. Ibid., 82.

7. See www.allianceforfairfood.org.

8. For a detailed description of cases in which CIW's efforts have successfully resisted the use of violence against agricultural workers, see www.ciw-online.org/slavery.html. Another form of direct action for citizens that has been quite effective is the fair trade movement, which seeks to rectify the inequalities of Third World farmers who receive only a pittance for their work. Most famous of these fair trade organizations is the giant Equal Exchange, whose products are sold over the Internet, in church basements, and in many other institutions. Some umbrella fair trade sites you can access include www.fairtrade-federation.org and www.fairtradecertified.org, or simply Google "fair trade" for particular products or locations.

9. See www.foodsresourcebank.org.

10. Tom Beaudoin, *Consuming Faith: Integrating Who We Are with What We Buy* (Lanham, Md.: Sheed & Ward, 2003), 94–95.

11. Penny Lauritzen, "Illinois Farms Share Thanksgiving Spirit with Guatamalans," in *Prairie Farmer* (December 2006). Found at www .foodsresourcebank.org/news.asp?id=280 <http://www.foodsresource bank.org/news.asp?id=280> .

Chapter 1

1. Dan Morgan, *Merchants of Grain* (New York: Penguin, 1980), 39, 216ff.

2. The 10 percent figure is from the Economic Research Service 2002 Food Consumer Price Index, Prices and Expenditures, Table 7, www.ers.usda.gov/Briefing/CPIFood and Expernditures/Data/table. htm. See also Southeast Farm Press, "State of U.S. Food Economy Fails to Prompt Quick Action," February 6, 2002, http://southeast-farmpress.com/ar/farming_state_us_farm/.

3. See R. J. Salvador and G. A. Zdorkowski, "Cheap Food That Isn't," www.public.iastate.edu/~rjsalvad/cheapfoodhtm. These figures are from 2001, but the relationship still holds.

4. N. Blisard, J. N. Variyam, and J. Cromartie, "Food Expenditures by U.S. Households: Looking Ahead to 2020," Economic Research Service, U.S. Department of Agriculture, Agricultural Economic Report No. 821, www.ers.usda.gov/publications/aer821/.

5. Salvador and Zdorkowski, "Cheap Food That Isn't."

6. www.idebate.org/database/topic_print.php?topicID=613.

7. *Online Etymology Dictionary*, www.etytmonline.com/index.php?term=complicity.

8. Bruno Fey and Alois Stutzer, *Happiness and Economics: How the Economy and Institutions Affect Well-Being* (Princeton: Princeton University Press, 2002), p. 74. Other economists agree that money cannot buy the most sought-after or cherished values.

9. See Deborah Kesten, *Feeding the Body, Nourishing the Soul* (Berkeley: Conari, 1977), for a compendium of how many faiths consider food and oppose hunger.

10. On the matter of how people relate to each other and approach possessions, see the threefold distinction of Miroslav Volf in *Free of Charge: On Giving and Forgiving in a Culture Stripped of Grace* (Grand Rapids: Zondervan, 2005), 56–57. He identifies three groups: the "takers," the "getters," and the "givers." (This typology was taken from Natalie Zemon Davies, *The Gift in Sixteenth-Century France* [Madison: University of Wisconsin Press, 2000], 9.) Takers are those who intend to benefit themselves whenever possible; this group views taking as commendable or at least okay religiously. For this group, then, appropriation would also be seen as morally commendable. The getters are achievement-oriented; they use legitimate, legal means to obtain what they want. They play by the rules and intend to succeed competitively in a way that is fair. This is the group that would

favor a meritocracy; that is, people should get what they deserve and work for. Exchange is the basis of the economy. The third group—the givers—are those who recognize the gifted quality of their lives and intend to share their gifts with others. They see life as somewhat gratuitous and whimsical, and thus feel free to give to others. Probably no one represents a 100 percent pure example of any of these three groups. However, in terms of the issue of appropriation, it is an interesting typology; appropriation fits pretty well into the category of takers, and somewhat less well into the category of getters. It would take a great effort to squeeze the act of appropriation into the category of givers in any way.

11. Kathryn Tanner, *Economy of Grace* (Minneapolis: Fortress Press, 2005), 28.

12. Ibid., 62.

13. John Koenig, *Holy Banquets: How Meals Become Mission in the Local Congregation* (Harrisburg, Pa.: Morehouse Publishing, 2007).

14. Tanner, *Economy of Grace*, 92–99.

15. I am using the word "myth" in two senses here. First, I mean that a myth is inaccurate, an untruth, but at the same time, an almost axiomatic belief in our culture. Second, in a quasi-religious sense, I mean that a myth, although untrue, is nevertheless powerfully alive and operative.

16. Barbara Kingsolver, *Animal, Vegetable, Miracle: A Year of Food Life* (New York: HarperCollins, 2007), chapter 13.

17. Victoria Spencer, "Farmers Markets Feed the 100-Mile Diet," CNN.com, September 4, 2007, www.cnn.com/2007/LIVING/wayoflife/08/31/buying.local.food/ (accessed February 19, 2009).

18. Tina Rosenberg, "Reverse Foreign Aid: Why Are Poor Countries Subsidizing Rich Ones?" *New York Times Magazine*, March 25, 2007, 16–19.

19. Ibid.

20. Ibid., 18.

Chapter 2

1. Michael Pollan, "The (Agri)Cultural Contradictions of Obesity," *New York Times Magazine*, October 12, 2003, 46.

2. Michael Pollan, "Unhappy Meals," *New York Times Magazine*, January 28, 2007, 38.

3. Ibid.

4. Prince Charles, "Agriculture: The Most Important of Humanity's Productive Activities," in *Manifestos on the Future of Food and Seed*, ed. Vandana Shiva (Cambridge, Mass.: South End Press, 2007), 28.

5. See Deborah Kesten, *Feeding the Body, Nourishing the Soul* (Berkeley: Conari, 1997), 7.

6. Stephanie Paulsell, *Honoring the Body: Meditations on a Christian Practice* (New York: Jossey-Bass, 2002.)

7. Mark Matousek, "Big Idea: Live Better with Less," *AARP The Magazine*, May–June 2007, www.aarpmagazine.org/lifestyle/bigidea_live_better_with_less.html/ (accessed February 15, 2009).

8. Corroborating and extending this thought found in Thomas Berry, *Evening Thoughts: Reflections on Earth as Sacred Community*, ed. Mary Evelyn Tucker (San Francisco: Sierra Club, 2006, is the work of Larry Rasmussen, *Earth Community, Earth Ethics* (Maryknoll, N.Y.: Orbis, 1996); Sallie McFague, *Life Abundant: Rethinking Theology and Economy for a Planet in Peril* (Minneapolis: Fortress Press, 2000) and *A New Climate for Theology* (Minneapolis: Fortress Press, 2008); Rosemary Radford Ruether, *Integrating Ecofeminism, Globalization, and World Religions* (New York: Rowman & Littlefield, 2005); and John Hart, *Sacramental Commons: Christian Ecological Ethics* (Lanham, Md.: Rowman & Littlefield, 2006).

9. See Kathryn Tanner, *Economy of Grace* (Minneapolis: Fortress Press, 2005), 92–99.

10. Tracy Kidder, *Mountain beyond Mountains* (New York: Random House, 2003.)

11. Quoted by David Bornstein, *How to Change the World: Social Entrepreneurs and the Power of New Ideas* (New York: Oxford, 2004), 126. Bornstein's work is the source of all the stories on pp. 53–55.

Chapter 3

1. Michael Pollan, "The Vegetable-Industrial Complex," *New York Times*, October 15, 2006, http://select.nytimes.com/preview/2006/10/15/magazine/ (accessed February 15, 2009).

2. Reported by Cathleen Hockman-Wert, "Check, Please! Our Long-Distance Food System Provides Choice—But at What Cost?" *Sojourners* 35, no. 5 (May 2006): 9.

3. See Andrew Kang Bartlett, "Energy, Food, and You," *Church & Society*, March–April 2004, 17–30.

4. Bob Herbert, "Poisoned on Eno Road," *New York Times*, October 2, 2006.

5. Kent A. Van Til, "Just Deserts: Beyond the Free Market," *Christian Century*, March 20, 2007, 21.

6. For a country-by-country listing of emissions, go to http:// timeforchange.org?/CO2-emissions-by-country.

7. Margaret Swedish, *Living beyond the "End of the World"* (Maryknoll, N.Y.: Orbis, 2008).

8. Alois Stutzer, "The Role of Income Aspirations in Individual Happiness," *Journal of Economic Behavior and Organization* 54 (2003): 89–109. It should be noted that the importance attached to aspirations is determined, I suspect, by the fact that the United States and Switzerland are affluent countries. See also Richard Layard, *Happiness: Lessons from a New Science* (New York: Penguin, 2005), 46.

9. Tim Kasser, *The High Price of Materialism* (Cambridge, Mass.: MIT Press, 2002), x.

10. Ibid., 5

11. Russell Belk, "Worldly Possessions: Issues and Criticism," in *Advances in Consumer Research*, vol. 10, ed. R. P. Bagozzi and A. M. Tybout (Ann Arbor, Mich.: Association for Consumer Research, 1983), 514–19; and Russell Belk, "Three Scales to Measure Constructs Related to Materialism: Reliability, Validity, and Relationship to Measures of Happiness," in *Advances in Consumer Research*, vol. 11, ed. T. Kinnear (Provo, Utah: Association for Consumer Research, 1984), 291–97.

12. In Rodney Clapp, *The Consuming Passion: Christianity and the Consumer Culture* (Downers Grove, Ill.: InterVarsity, 1998).

13. David Myers, "Money and Misery," in Clapp, *Consuming Passion*, 64.

14. Larry Rasmussen, "Creating the Commons," in *Justice in a Global Economy: Strategies for Home, Community, and World*, ed. Pamela Brubaker, Rebecca Todd Peters, and Laura Stivers (Louisville, Ky.: Westminster John Knox, 2006), 101.

15. W. Anne Joh, "Relating to Household Labor Justly," in Brubaker, Peters, and Stivers, *Justice in a Global Economy*, 35.

16. Gary T. Gardner, *Inspiring Progress: Religions' Contribution to Sustainable Development* (New York: W. W. Norton, 2006), 46–47, 57.

Chapter 4

1. Michael Grunwald, "Down on the Farm," *Time*, November 12, 2007, 28–36.

2. The Department of Agriculture Economic Research Service of the U.S. released these figures in its February 5, 2009, report of the U.S. Farm Census made for the year 2007. See www.ers.usda.gov (accessed February 10, 2009) http://www.agcensus.usda.gov/Publications/2007/Full_Report/Volume_1,_Chapter_1_US/st99_1_002_002.pdf. Another source suggests that farms with sales of $500,000 or more made up only 3 percent of all farms but accounted for 52 percent of production. http://www.agcensus.usda.gov/Publications/2007/Online_Highlights/Fact_Sheets/farm_numbers.pdf. See also James McDonald, Robert Hoppe, and David Banker, "Growing Farm Size and the Distribution of Farm Payment," USDA ERS, Economic Brief Number 6, March 2006, p. 2.

3. Ibid.

4. An interesting comment buried in an article on the debate over the Farm Bill suggested that no one should be called a "farmer" unless they obtain at least two-thirds of their income from farming operations (*Kansas City Star*, December 14, 2007). There would not be many farmers in this country according to that definition.

5. McDonald, Hoppe, and Banker, "Growing Farm Size and the Distribution of Farm Payments," 2.

6. Vincent A. Gallagher, *The True Cost of Low Prices: The Violence of Globalization* (Maryknoll, N.Y.: Orbis, 2006), 82.

7. Eric Schlosser, "One Thing to Do about Food," a forum edited by Alice Waters, *The Nation* 283, no. 1 (September 11, 2006): 14.

8. Bob Herbert, "Where the Hogs Come First," *New York Times*, June 15, 2006, op-ed.

9. Bread for the World press release, "Bread for the World Reaction to Senate Agriculture Committee Proposal on the Farm Bill,"

October 25, 2007, http://www.bread.org/press-room/releases/bread
-for-the-world-reaction-to-senate-agriculture-committee-proposal-
on-the-farm-bill.html
    10. http://www.cipa-apex.org/toomuch/tmweekly.html
    11. Ibid.
    12. David Bornstein, *How to Change the World: Social Entrepre-neurs and the Power of New Ideas* (New York: Oxford, 2004), 16.
    13. Albino Barrera, *Economic Compulsion and Christian Ethics* (Cambridge: Cambridge University Press, 2005), 103.
    14. Jeffrey D. Sachs, "What a Little Fertilizer Can Do," *Time*, August 6, 2007, 54.
    15. The story of Fabio Rosa on which I have drawn extensively is from David Bornstein, "The Light in My Head Went On—Fabio Rosa, Brazil: Rural Electrification," in *How to Change the World*, (New York: Oxford University Press, 2007), 20–39.

Chapter 5

    1. My thanks to my colleague Dr. Jeanne Hoeft for trying to help me understand Butler.
    2. Richard Layard, *Happiness: Lessons from a New Science* (New York: Penguin, 2005), 226, 230, 231, 232–35. Here he recommends moral education in schools, as well as policies to build stable families, communities, and workplaces. "We should spend more on helping the poor, on tackling the problem of mental illness, on improving family life and on activities that promote community life. We should eliminate high unemployment, fight against the constant escalation of wants (by prohibiting advertisement to children) and education for social moral-ity." Ibid., 232–35.
    3. See James Konow and Joseph Earley, "The Hedonistic Paradox: Is Homo Economicus Happier?" *Journal of Public Economics* 92, nos. 1–2 (2008): 1–33.
    4. They cite numerous other experimental results, among them Gary Charness and Brit Grosskopf, "Relative Payoffs and Happiness: An Experimental Study," *Journal of Economic Behavior and Orga-nization* 45, no. 3 (2001): 301–28; John Helliwell, "Well-Being, Social Capital, and Public Policy: What's New?" *Economic Journal* (2006);

Sonja Lyubomirsky, Kennon Sheldon, and David Schkade, "Pursuing Happiness: The Architecture of Sustainable Change," *Review of General Psychology* 9, no. 2 (2005): 111–31.

5. Peggy Thoits and Lyndi Hewitt, "Volunteer Work and Well-Being," *Journal of Health and Social Behavior* 42, no. 2 (2001): 115–31.

6. "It's Better to Give," *Christian Century*, January 29, 2008, 9.

7. Charles Mathewes, "On Using the World," in *Having: Property and Possession in Religious and Social Life*, ed. William Schweiker and Charles Mathewes (Grand Rapids: Eerdmans, 2004), 189-190.

8. Ibid., 199.

9. "John Chrysostom: You Are Possessed by Possessions," in *Ownership: Early Christian Teaching*, ed. Charles Avila (Maryknoll, N.Y.: Orbis, 1983), quoted in David Matzko McCarthy, *The Good Life: Genuine Christianity for the Middle Class* (Grand Rapids: Brazos, 2004), 111.

10. Ambrose, "Born Naked," in Avila, *Ownership*, ibid.

11. Kathryn Tanner, *Economy of Grace* (Minneapolis: Fortress Press, 2005), 73.

12. Ibid., 75.

13. Kenneth R. Himes, "Consumerism and Christian Ethics," *Theological Studies* 68 (2007): 153. See the whole article, 132–53.

14. Craig Nessan, *Give Us This Day: A Lutheran Response to World Hunger* (Minneapolis: Fortress Press, 2003). See chapters 3 and 4.

15. Monica K. Hellwig, *The Eucharist and the Hunger of the World*, 2nd ed. (Franklin, WI: Sheed & Ward, 1992), 13-14, 80-81.

Chapter 6

1. Perhaps Marjorie Thompson, *Soul Feast: Christian Disciplines* (Louisville, Ky.: Westminster John Knox, 1995), and Dorothy C. Bass, ed., *Practicing the Faith: A Way of Life for a Searching People* (San Francisco: Jossey-Bass, 1997), were the first contemporary books leading this movement. Since that time, there has been a series of books on practices from Jossey-Bass, including Stephanie Paulsell, *Honoring the Body: Meditations on a Christian Practice* (2002), and Dorothy Bass, *Receiving the Day: Christian Practices for Opening the Gift of*

Time (2000). Marva Dawn offers a helpful and extensive list of these in her *Unfettered Hope: A Call to Faithful Living in an Affluent Society* (Louisville, Ky.: Westminster, 2003), 180–81. Closer to our topic, see David Matzko McCarthy, *The Good Life: Genuine Christianity for the Middle Class* (Eugene, Ore.: Wipf & Stock, 2006); Kenneth R. Himes, "Moral Notes: Consumerism," *Theological Studies* 68, March 2007; Kent Van Til, *Less Than Two Dollars a Day: A Christian View of World Poverty and the Free Market* (Grand Rapids: Eerdmans, 2007).

2. Vincent Miller, *Consuming Religion: Christian Faith and Practices in a Consumer Culture* (New York: Continuum, 2004), 12.

3. Marilyn Chandler McEntyre, "Too Much with Us," *Weavings* 19, no. 5 (September–October 2004): 40.

4. A study by Kathleen Vohs, reported in *Science*, found that the presence of money in a person's environment, including simply images of money on a screen saver, makes people reach out for help less often and give less help to others who reach out to them. People also physically distance themselves more from others. The mere presence of money itself results in more isolation, which, of course, is the opposite of what God wants from us in the kingdom.

5. See Barbara Kingsolver, *Animal, Vegetable, Miracle: A Year of Food Life* (New York: HarperCollins, 2007), and Bill McKibben, *Deep Economy: The Wealth of Communities and the Durable Future* (New York: Times Books/Henry Holt, 2007).

6. McKibben, *Deep Economy*, 35.

7. Penny Lauritzen, "Illinois Farms Share Thanksgiving Spirit with Guatemalans," *Prairie Farmer*, December 2006, 54.

8. Eric Holt-Gimenez, "The Whole Food Crisis: What's behind It and What We Can Do about It," in Food First: Institute for Food and Development Policy, "Policy Brief No. 16," October 2008, 13, www.foodfirst.org.

INDEX

Abundance 1-5, 8, 20, 22, 27-30, 32, 84, 116, 129

Accountability 22, 96, 111, 122, 130

Acknowledgement 16, 24-25, 102, 117

Affluence/Affluent 1, 3, 6- 9, 15-17, 23, 25, 45, 50-51, 54, 66, 70, 81, 85, 94-95, 98-99, 111, 125, 129, 132

Affordability 18, 19, 23, 26, 43, 49, 91, 126, 133

AIDS/HIV 22, 53-54, 56

Appropriate/Appropriation 15, 16, 22-27, 30-31, 33-34, 37, 44-46, 51, 57, 63, 70, 81-82, 85, 96, 102, 104, 109-111, 115, 117-118, 120-122, 124-125, 128, 135, 137

Awareness 33-35, 68, 117-118, 123

Blindness 22, 30, 64, 96

Bread for the World 38, 80, 131

Buddha/Buddhism 5, 53, 72, 93, 122, 128

Calvin, John 28, 103, 105, 109

Change 8, 13, 16-17, 19, 54, 64, 67, 75, 82, 89-93, 105, 118-119, 122-127, 130-134, 137

Cheap Food 7, 10, 15-23, 25, 27, 29, 31-38, 42, 75, 77, 80-82, 93, 122

Christian/Christianity 5, 22, 26-28, 31-32, 35, 44-45, 47, 67-68, 72, 85, 93, 99 100, 103-104, 107, 109, 115. 117-120, 128, 130

Chrysostom, John 102-103, 105

Commodity 17, 20, 23, 43, 62, 76, 81, 88

Communion/Eucharist 6, 47, 85, 105, 108-110, 112, 119

Community 10-13, 33, 36-37, 47-48, 56-58, 61, 63-64, 67-69, 71-75, 77-78, 80-89, 91, 93, 99, 103, 105, 107, 116, 118-119, 123-124, 126-127, 129, 131-132, 137

Compassion 16, 22, 68-69, 110, 127-128, 130

Complicity 1, 6-7, 9, 13, 15-16, 20-22, 24, 33-35, 37, 43, 45-46,

62-64, 67, 79, 95-100, 117, 135-137

Confess/Confession 15, 34-35, 117-118

Consumer/ism 10, 17-18, 33, 35, 44-45, 58, 63-66, 88, 91, 102, 106, 109-110, 119-122, 125, 132

Consumption 4, 20, 45-46, 51-54, 62, 64-67, 93, 95, 101, 108-110, 115, 117, 119, 121-122, 126

Control 20, 45, 76, 86, 88-89, 94-95

Daoism 53, 85, 93

Diet 43-44, 52, 57, 61-62, 120, 125, 133

Disease 22, 43-44, 51, 54-55, 59, 95, 104, 120-121, 125-126, 137

Distribution 1, 5, 17, 20-21, 33, 48-50, 56, 60-62, 70-71, 85-86, 88-83, 103

Economic 1-4, 16, 19, 21, 30, 32, 34, 37, 44, 48, 51, 67, 72-73, 82, 84, 86, 90-91, 98, 105, 108, 130, 133, 137

Embody 30, 118, 120, 123

Enjoyment 32-33, 85, 95, 105, 119, 129

Environment 19, 21, 36, 58, 61-62, 64, 70, 72, 75, 79-80, 84, 87, 90-91, 93, 109, 116, 126-127, 133

Fair Trade 37, 137

Faith 3 -6, 8, 13, 26-27, 32-34, 53, 56, 73, 89, 100, 128

Farm Workers 10-11, 23, 59, 79-80, 84, 86-87, 89-91

Fasting 119-122

Food Policy 7, 16-18, 20, 23, 27, 29-33, 35, 38, 42, 44, 75, 77-78, 80, 87, 93, 122, 131

Food Resource Bank (FRB) 11-12

Forgive 34-35, 102, 111, 117, 136-137

Generosity/Generous 2, 37, 56, 65, 73, 98, 106, 110, 121, 128

Giving 5, 28-30, 33, 47, 49, 75, 98-99, 103-108, 121-122, 127-130, 136

Global Warming 17, 22, 57, 59, 68

Globalization 21, 31, 49

God 2-8, 27-35, 44-45, 47-50, 53, 68-70, 72, 83-86, 91, 94, 100-112, 116-122, 124, 128, 136-137

Gratitude 2, 12, 35, 104, 108-109, 128-129

Guilt 21

Happiness 2, 4-8, 13, 16, 24-25, 32, 43, 45-46, 51-52, 57, 63-66, 81-83, 94, 96-101, 111-112, 116, 121-123, 126, 128, 136

Health Care 2, 48-52, 56, 79, 104, 132-133

Health/Healthy 2, 15, 19, 36, 41-56, 58-59, 61, 63-66, 71, 78-79, 81-82, 86-87, 91, 99-101, 104, 121, 123, 126, 130, 132-133

Hindu 44, 53, 72, 119

Hospitality 105, 119, 121-122

Hunger 1, 3-8, 11-13, 15-16, 20, 24, 27-28, 34, 38, 46, 53, 55-56, 77, 91, 94, 104, 111, 115-118, 120, 124, 130, 131, 137

Immigrants/Migrants 10, 23, 32, 79, 120

Individualism/Individualistic 47, 52, 64, 67, 69, 96

Inequalities 48, 81

Injustice 8-9, 26, 35, 38, 81, 137

Interconnect 41, 51, 67-70, 93, 100

Intimacy 66, 127

Islam 5, 19, 93

Jesus 5, 27-28, 48, 53, 70, 107, 110,
    117-118, 122, 124, 135-137
Judaism 5, 53, 72, 93
Justice 32, 49-50, 61, 70-71, 83-86,
    110, 130
    Distributive 49-50, 70, 85-86
    Sustainable 50, 70
    Restorative 50, 70
    Contributive 50, 85
Lifestyle 24, 45, 48, 51, 53, 56,
    63, 72, 94, 95, 108, 117, 123,
    125-126
Luther, Martin 28
Luxury 34, 70, 119
Malnutrition 7, 46, 72, 104, 131
Materialistic 65-66, 102, 117
McKibben, Bill 66, 124, 126
Moral/Morally 13, 21, 24-25, 27,
    31-33, 37, 49, 69, 85, 101-102,
    105, 108-112, 117
Nutrition 35, 42-44, 54, 61, 88
Obesity/Overweight 43, 45-47, 51,
    52, 54, 82, 120, 125, 126
Political 1, 2, 4, 9, 17, 18, 20, 32,
    67, 72, 76, 86, 90, 99, 130
Pollan, Michael 42-43
Poor/Poverty 1, 4, 5, 7-12, 18, 21,
    23, 25, 37-38, 43-44, 46, 54, 56,
    63, 77-82, 88, 93, 97, 102-106,
    109-111, 115-118, 124, 129-
    131, 133, 136-137
Possession 1, 4, 65, 82, 102-103,
    106, 137
Production/ Overproduction 1,
    17, 19, 42, 44, 58, 59, 62-64,
    71, 76, 79, 84, 86, 89-90, 133
Reality 3, 6, 21, 26, 30-31, 46, 57,
    69, 84, 95, 115, 116, 117, 133
Relationship 12, 26, 30, 34-36, 44,
    50, 66, 67, 70-71, 75, 88, 94,
    96, 98, 100, 103, 106, 107, 109,
    112, 116, 123, 127, 129
Repentance 35, 117-118

Rural Communities 75-80, 82-87,
    89, 91, 93
Saint Ambrose 103, 105, 106
Saint Francis of Assisi 122, 128
Sanctification 35, 118
Scarcity 3-4, 71, 129
Second Harvest 38, 56
Self-examination 117, 118, 120, 121
Shalom 47, 69, 83, 84, 100, 102
Sharing 5, 12, 24-25, 27, 47, 85, 89,
    102-103, 105, 107-108, 112,
    119-122, 127-129
Sin 17, 18, 28- 31, 34, 48, 96, 100-
    101
Spiritual 17, 12-13, 24, 27, 44, 47,
    54, 64, 67, 72, 93-96, 100, 105-
    106, 116, 120, 125, 128, 135
Starvation 1, 22, 33, 72, 87, 94, 104,
    110-111
Subsidy 17, 19-21, 37, 38, 43, 44,
    46, 78, 81, 86, 87, 132, 133
Suffer 1, 3, 5, 7-8, 12, 15-16, 22-25,
    27, 33, 46, 48, 63, 66, 67, 71,
    83-84, 106, 110-111, 127-128,
    131, 137
Sustainability 68, 70-71, 82, 110
Tanner, Kathryn 28, 32, 49, 103, 105
Transform 12, 33, 35, 51, 71, 80,
    87, 106, 115, 117, 118, 127,
    129, 130, 136
Unhappiness 6, 24, 46, 65, 101, 136
Volunteer 12, 99, 121, 123, 136
Waste 19, 21, 53, 58, 61-62, 72
Wealth/Wealthy 4-5, 7, 12, 23, 25,
    37, 45, 51, 53, 65, 66, 89, 103,
    106-107, 124, 128-130
Wellbeing 2, 4, 6-7, 12-13, 16,
    23-26, 33, 35-36, 46, 49-52,
    63-64, 66-67, 69-71, 81-83, 86,
    95-99, 101-102, 109-112, 116,
    118, 122, 127-128, 130, 133,
    135-137
Wholeness 47-48, 69, 101, 136